✻ PRAISE FOR *GRACE:* A MODEL FOR GRIEVING

"With straightforward language accessible to clinicians and clients, *GRACE: A Model for Grieving* provides practical exercises to change the relationship between self and grief. Dr. Kay Towns has given practitioners the *gift* of a stepwise approach to addressing the overlooked aspects of culture and spirituality in the treatment of grief."
—Dawn Ellison, DPC, LPC, former director of Doctor of Professional Counseling Program, Mississippi College

"These practical techniques provide the grieving individual the needed steps to create hope in their life when dealing with devastating loss. *GRACE: A Model for Grieving* is a go-to grief handbook for the bereaved, licensed mental health practitioners, and clergy and spiritual leaders."
—Rev. Jerry L. Terrill DSM, LPC-S, LMFT-S

"*GRACE: A Model for Grieving* is a gift to anyone on the journey of grief. The comprehensive model offers five practical tools to create insight and healing. Each person's unique and individual experience of grief is treated holistically, offering a pathway of growth through loss."
—Dr. Lorna Bradley, author of *Special Needs Parenting*

"The 'GRACE Grief Model' is a masterpiece that offers a new perspective on grief by blending well-known, evidence-based therapeutic theories into a singular model. *GRACE: A Model for Grieving* is groundbreaking, compressible, and shines a light on the human experience of grief. Anyone who has experienced loss or who works with individuals who are experiencing loss will find this book to be an invaluable resource."
—Rayan Al Jurdi, MD

GRACE:
A Model for Grieving

GRACE:
A Model for Grieving

A Five-Step Guide for
Healing After Loss

KAY TOWNS, DPC, LPC

Foreword by Lauren Marangell, MD

Hatherleigh Press is committed to preserving
and protecting the natural resources of the earth.
Environmentally responsible and sustainable practices
are embraced within the company's mission statement.

Visit us at hatherleighpress.com and register online
for free offers, discounts, special events, and more.

GRACE: A MODEL FOR GRIEVING

Text Copyright © 2024 Dr. Kay Towns

Library of Congress Cataloging-in-Publication Data is available.

ISBN: 978-1-57826-997-6

Printed in the United States

10 9 8 7 6 5 4 3 2 1

This book is dedicated to the many patients who have shared their
struggles with grief with me. Also, thank you to my family—Kirk,
Ryan, and Davis—for their patience, support, and love, which
I especially leaned on during the years it took me to write this book.

*Waves of loss ebb and flow throughout our lives,
but within these murky waters hope floats. In each new wave of grief,
we find opportunity to heal. In our sorrow we are presented a
chance to feel, to name, and to learn from our wounded places.
Among the brokenness, we can find the gift grieving brings—
the opening to move from pain to peace, from heartbreak to hope.*

�֍ CONTENTS

✳ FOREWORD

A S A TENURED PROFESSOR of psychiatry with a specialty in depression, I have seen thousands of patients struggling with loss. While excellent psychotherapy modalities exist to help despair in many therapeutic areas, there exists a clear gap in therapies to meet the needs of patients who are suffering from grief.

GRACE: A Model for Grieving by Dr. Kay Towns is an important new work to help both clinicians and patients through these periods of life. Dr. Towns takes the tools from cognitive behavioral therapy (CBT) and expands these concepts, noting that grief is not a problem to be solved but a healing process. The "problem" is the loss itself.

The structure of the book is logical: starting with a modern understanding of grief (including a neurobiological model), Dr. Towns proceeds to outline a 5-step model to facilitate healing. The key to this model is her view that healing in grief is *innate*, much like the innate physical healing of the body. Pain is not ignored or minimized; emotions are acknowledged and honored; individuals are given the opportunity to convalesce, rather than the expectation that they immediately "bounce back."

GRACE: A Model for Grieving is accessible to both patients and clinicians and is a must-read for therapists who treat people who are grieving. The book addresses grief beyond the loss of life and includes grief from other sources, such as the loss of a job or an important relationship. While the concept of "waves of grief" is not new, Dr. Towns does an excellent job enhancing this metaphor with a simple schematic, one which motivates people to *stay* with their painful feelings when the agonizing waves come rather than trying to block them or distract themselves with work or alcohol—a delaying process that only serves to create a tsunami somewhere down the line.

I was most intrigued by her presentation of how a person's worldview may or may not align with their view of the loss at hand. Grief is more likely to result in growth when these factors are aligned and more likely to lead to chronic trauma when they are not. Her key insight is that the worldview itself is not the salient issue, it is the *alignment* (or lack thereof) that effects the healing process. In my experience, this is therapeutic work for many, and Dr. Towns' presentation is both unique and pragmatic.

I expect that any reader will enjoy reading *GRACE: A Model for Grieving* from cover to cover. It provides an extremely useful framework for interventions to help reframe grief as a reparative process.

—Lauren Marangell, MD
    Clinical Professor of Psychiatry, UT McGovern Medical School
    Co-Founder, Brain Health Consultants

✳ INTRODUCTION

MARCUS WAS 18 WHEN his twin brother died by suicide. After the tragedy, Marcus found himself in deep mourning while at the same time preparing to leave for college. Marcus simultaneously faced a beginning and an end; he would start his exciting new college life but in a state of despair, crestfallen by the profound absence of his brother. His stability, his world, and his faith had been shaken and Marcus sometimes felt as if his feet might not ever find solid ground again.

Robert thought he had it all—good health, an active fun lifestyle, great family and friends, and a prosperous career. When he first was diagnosed with Covid, his symptoms seemed mild, so he did not think much of it. However, as the virus progressed inside him, he grew increasingly ill and was hospitalized. The virus nearly took Robert's life and even after recovery, Covid left him with debilitating long-term physical problems and a cascade of mounting emotional struggles.

Sheila received her second lay-off slip in three years, especially difficult given the current economic recession and mounting costs of caring for her child with special needs. She worried she would not find another job soon enough and agonized over how she was going to pay rent or afford her child's prescription medications. People like Marcus, Robert, and Sheila, come to me with struggles expressing many emotions regarding the losses they feel. While each person's situations and emotions vary, there exists a prevailing and almost palpable commonality present in almost everyone I meet with: people feel overwhelmed and almost everyone is grieving something.

Feeling overwhelmed is understandable given the challenges and formidable circumstances that many are facing. At the time of completing this book, our world seems to be in a state of suspended collective and individual grief. At a macro level, concerns are fueled by wars and conflicts, lingering effects of the COVID-19 pandemic, global political and social unrest, racial and gender injustices, and devastating natural disasters, all of which take center stage on the nightly news and social media feeds. At the same time, families and individuals are pained with personal losses, including deaths and illness of loved ones, financial woes from job loss and inflation, rising healthcare costs amidst increasingly limited access to medical care and needed medications, and relationship strains from compounding stressors and a culture that struggles to speak with civility to anyone with opposing views.

These difficulties can feel crushing for many and create a revolving door of loss-after-loss resulting in what feels like an untethering, all the while, our physical and mental selves try to absorb blow after blow. The subsequent individual and communal mental distress exacts a heavy toll personally and collectively. In a time of elevated sense of loss, we could all benefit from additional adaptive resources targeted to address losses and the accompanying grief. I am grateful to be able to offer a new type of hope needed by many in the form of an evidenced-based approach to grief and loss, the GRACE Grief Model™.

Grief affects every person at some point in their life individually and communally. Grief in its severe form is known as prolonged grief (formerly known as complicated grief), which is when the difficult emotions of loss are severe and do not improve over time. Prolonged grief has recently made its way into the *Diagnostic and Statistical Manual of Mental Disorders*[1] as "Persistent Complex Bereavement Disorder (PCBD)," and has been deemed a health hazard with potentially life-threating implications.

---

[1] American Psychiatric Association, 2013

Further, Prolonged Grief Disorder (PGD) has also recently made its way into the DSM-5-TR (APA, 2020). This disorder, like PCBD, is limited to grief related to bereavement. While there are similarities between PCBD and PGD, there remain characteristics unique to each, thus the need for two separate diagnoses (of note, there are those who argue there is "no substantive difference between PGD and PCBD)."[2]

Solid evidence continues to affirm cognitive behavioral therapy's (CBT) general effectiveness in treating mental health conditions.[3] However, a problem exists in that current grief-related treatment models have been found to be lacking, including CBT which is presently recognized as the most efficacious model for grief treatment. Literature has suggested for decades that CBT in-general has limitations.[4] Further, CBT alone offers incomplete treatment for grief, which has long since stirred calls for CBT's continued refinement.[5]

While immensely helpful in the treatment of grief, CBT alone falls short of fully addressing the suffering of grief. Four ways in which CBT when used alone proves lacking in the treatment of grief stem from the following: 1. An emphasis on trying to identify something as a "problem," 2. Lack of cultural and ethical considerations including pluralistic identities, 3. Lack of meaning-making inclusive of spirituality, and 4. Limitations when logic and rational thought are difficult to achieve. In grief, the "problem" commonly is loss itself, as in cases of bereavement. It is often not someone's illogical thinking, unprocessed feelings, or unhealthy behaviors that caused the "problem" in most grief situations. With grief,

---

[2] Maciejewski, Maercker, Boelen, Prigerson, 2016

[3] David, Cristea, & Holmann, 2018

[4] Holmes, 2002; Morin 2002; Goldberg 1998; Cuijpers, van Straten, Andersson, & van Oppen, 2008; Baardseth et al., 2013; Ali et al., 2017; Ratnayake & Poppe, 2020

[5] Neimeyer & Currier, 2009

it is primarily the loss itself that is the cause. For example, soon after Mary's mother died, Mary began to spiral into depression mixed with anxiety. In the weeks after her mother's death, Mary's thoughts at times were illogical and even her memory often seemed impaired. However, for Mary these were due to grief and not some pathological process. Loss, although painful and with real impacts on our mind and body, is a normal part of our human condition. The grief that follows does not automatically equate to a problem that must be named or necessarily pathologized (a diagnosis of prolonged grief being the exception), but rather loss refers to a normal and inevitable part of our humanness.

The CBT model of therapy relies heavily on the therapist's competence and preparation. CBT's inherent ethical challenges include a counselor's training, or lack thereof, to address epistemic failure and determine what is or is not rational cognition.[6] Further, CBT seems to omit cultural consideration, multidimensional identities, and meaning-making (including spirituality). CBT framing and research has been focused on European Americans, "with little to no attention given to cultural influences related to ethnicity, religion, sexual orientation, disability, or social class."[7]

CBT alone for the treatment of grief can prove problematic because, while CBT hinges on identifying and replacing illogical or irrational thought, the thoughts that accompany grief can often be just that—illogical or irrational. Grief can impact our neurobiology, and grief events can create literal changes to our brain and chemistry. These changes may make achieving rational and logical thought very difficult at times. However, when using CBT alone, rational and logical thought are needed for successful CBT results. So, as in the case of a severe initial grief reaction (e.g., when a loved one dies suddenly) until a grieving person is biologically capable of rational and logical thought, CBT therapy can stall.

---

[6] Ratnayake & Poppe, 2020

[7] Iwamasa & Hayes, 2019, p. 5

Psychologist Dr. Stefan Hofmann, in writing about the future of CBT, states that "(e)ffective CBT has to target all aspects of human suffering."[8] I agree and believe this should extend to the suffering caused by grief. But for CBT to extend its reach effectively into the treatment of grief, modifications are needed. My approach towards tackling this problem was to lean firmly into CBT's known strengths while filling in the gaps by incorporating adaptations of complementary therapy (I chose narrative therapy) within a meaning-making (inclusive of spirituality) framework.

I created the GRACE Grief Model out of necessity. As an ordained United Methodist minister (order of deacon) and Licensed Professional Counselor, my work with others has often centered on loss. In my prior grief work with clients and patients, I tried without success to find an evidenced-based model of grief that supports a person's individualized loss journey while also incorporating spirituality and meaning-making. It is from my need to find a more comprehensive grief model in hopes of better helping others through their loss that my passion developed to create a new approach to grief work, giving birth to the GRACE Grief Model.

In this model, the restorative gift of grief is highlighted and affirmed. At its core, the GRACE Grief Model promotes healthy grieving and offers an evidenced-based opportunity to help grow and heal through loss recovery and restoration, including constructing meaning from our loss as we move forward in our grief process. The GRACE Grief Model presents grief as a gift and reparative renewal as the process through which regeneration and growth begin. Within the grief process is an invitation to repair from loss and heal loss wounds. Scripture reminds us that God does not allow pain without allowing something new to be born (Jeremiah 66:9). The reparative process of grieving enables this new

---

[8] Dr. Stefan Hoffman, 2021, p. 383

growth and invites us to develop new and healthier ways of thinking, feeling, and behaving. Through this model, adaptive grief work invites cathartic constructivism (catharsis based on an individual's own experiences) for effectual healing.

The GRACE Grief Model uses elements of CBT along with elements of narrative therapy within a framework that supports individual beliefs, goals, and sense of purpose (meaning-making inclusive of spirituality). My goal in creating this model is to offer an alternative grief treatment aimed at facilitating the grieving process and expanding grief treatment options to help more people. I was elated to observe the effectiveness of the GRACE Grief Model first-hand. As I worked in the hospital setting and in private practice, I found incorporating aspects of the GRACE Grief Model into individual and group therapies successfully supported patients healing from loss, even for patients stalled in their grieving process or struggling with prolonged grief. Within my practice, I regularly witness how the GRACE Grief Model provides a new system of support that other grief models lack, helping to more effectively treat a broader grieving population.

Prior to the creation of the GRACE Grief Model, many existing grief models included CBT and CBT-based approaches, and also narrative therapy and narrative-based approaches. However, I was unable to locate a model that integrated CBT and narrative therapy within a meaning-making framework supporting individual beliefs, goals, and sense of purpose. The GRACE Grief Model achieves this and promotes a model of grief work that is biologically imperative, emotionally healing, and spiritualty nurturing. Further, the GRACE model moves past just treating symptoms, which is the primary aim of CBT, and allows for a new understanding and relationship with grief.

Of note, while I have my own personal beliefs and ways of relating to the Divine, my religious views are not highlighted in this book given the purpose of this text is to provide grief support to a broad population and, in doing so, value the uniqueness of each person's personal spiritual journey. I acknowledge here that because of my faith education and spiritual formation, many of the examples and illustrations I pull from and offer in this text do lean towards a Christian perspective, however, my intent is not to be exclusive or alienate anyone with different religious or spiritual understandings.

Again, this book is intended for people who have been struggling with grief, and specifically offers a complementary resource for those who are in grief counseling. This book is also intended for grief educators, psychotherapists, and mental healthcare professionals.

This work depicts many years of personal and professional work and dedication towards helping people grieve in healthier ways. To illustrate the actual work of grieving, I have added numerous stories, including several personal stories about me and my family. I sincerely hope you find this book and the GRACE Grief Model helpful as you move through your own grief journey.

Disclaimers

In this book, only personal stories about me and my family are factual; all other stories and names in this work are fictional representations (scenarios) intended to represent actual cases for informational and illustration purposes. My decision not to include my clients'/patients' stories was made out of an abundance of caution to protect client/patient identities and their information. Any potential similarity in these scenario stories to real life are purely coincidental and are not based on any actual persons. I also note here, I was trained as a counselor in the hospital setting and subsequently practiced counseling professionally in a medical setting. Therefore, I often use the term "patient" rather than client to refer to those whom I have counseled and those I currently counsel.

Importantly, to further support you along your grief journey, I have created an additional resource, *GRACE: A Model for Grieving Workbook*, to serve as a complementary tool to this handbook. This GRACE Workbook expands on the information within this text and offers a wealth of supportive tools and exercises that align with the GRACE Grief Model™ to move you even further towards health and healing.

✳ HOW TO USE THIS BOOK

THIS BOOK IS INTENDED for people who have been struggling with grief, including those with prolonged grief (also known as complicated grief). This work is designed as a complementary resource for patients and clients in grief counseling, and also serves as a useful tool to guide grief educators, psychotherapists, and mental healthcare workers.

CHAPTERS 1 & 2

The first two chapters provide a high-level academically focused overview of grief and the GRACE Grief Model. These initial chapters present detailed physiological and educational information regarding grief. This level of depth is offered to provide not only a traditional interpretation of what grief is, but also to walk you through a more contemporary biological understanding of grief.

CHAPTERS 3–7

The next five chapters of this book offer a five-step process for grieving. These chapters showcase elements of the GRACE Grief Model, providing a new way to heal from loss. Each chapter will focus on a different process: Step 1. Grief redefined, Step 2. Re-story the loss narrative, Step 3. Adopt healthy ways to grieve, Step 4. Connect with self and others, and Step 5. Engage in a "new normal" within a livable pattern of grief work.

CHAPTER 8

The final chapter extends support for how to move forward within the "new normal." Adopting healthy grief work into the rhythm of our life promotes ongoing healing from loss. Grief then becomes something we no longer avoid or minimize, but rather an honored part of how we live and a holistic recognition of who we are as a humankind tethered to loss.

Chapter 1

ABOUT GRIEF

"The weight of the loss feels so heavy, like a boulder sitting on my chest pulling me under."

—CATRINA, GRIEVING PATIENT

WHAT IS GRIEF?

When I ask people what grief is, they most often reply by describing how they *feel*. The feelings, after all, are at the core of our perceived grief experience. While there are other forms of grief expression, including physical, behavioral, and cognitive, grief is first and foremost an emotion, which I will explain later in this chapter. Our human condition seems hard-wired to feel life's losses, to feel those aches and pains, feelings which can be experienced individually and collectively.

Ingrained in our very creation within our DNA seems to be a mechanism for managing life's losses in a way that organically promotes feelings and healing, and this mechanism is the natural and ongoing process we call grieving. While many attest grief work has a beginning, a middle, and an end, I regard the work on grief as ongoing cycles that, like waves, will continue to ebb and flow in and out of our lives without a final ending demarcation. For example, decades after I grieved and healed from a loss, something may trigger a memory and I find myself presented once again with an opportunity to re-grieve that same loss.

Importantly, there is a distinction between ongoing adaptive (healthy) grief work and grief that is prolonged or severe (unhealthy), so when I state grief should be ongoing, I am referring to the healthy process of grief work, which is vastly different from maladaptive prolonged grief. The GRACE Grief Model supports healthy ongoing grief work while helping address unhealthy grieving, including prolonged grief. This will be explored more in later chapters.

The process of grieving, and especially learning to grieve in healthy ways, not only makes us feel better, but it is also essential and primary for our human survival.[1] Yet, grief has a bit of a reputation problem; most consider grief as something unwanted and to be rushed through or, worse, avoided altogether. However, in this book I hope to dispel stigma around grief and create a deeper understanding of grief's amazingly beautiful healing role in our lives. I aim to help redefine grief for you as biologically imperative, emotionally healing, and spiritually nurturing.

DEFINITIONS: LOSS, GRIEF, AND GRIEVING

Whereas loss refers to an *event* (such as a death, illness, job layoff, divorce, etc.), grief refers to our *reaction* to the loss event. Grief is "the emotion of loss,"[2] and affects a person's cognitive (thoughts), emotional (feelings), and behavioral (actions) responses.[3] Grief impacts our whole being—our physical self, our mental self, and the very actions we take or do not take. The work of processing our grief, which focuses on the feelings and emotions of loss, is known as grieving.

---

[1] Pena-Vargas, Armaiz-Pena, Castro-Figueroa, 2021
[2] Scheff, 2015, p. 458
[3] Shear, 2011

GRIEF'S "TIMELINE"

Grieving itself is an individual process. While grief can impact us collectively and be processed collectively to some extent, each person will react to loss and their emotions around loss in different ways and along their own body's timeline. Many have been raised believing grief must be dealt with quickly, often a result of cultural minimization of the grieving process. Quite simply, too many feel uncomfortable with the grief process. However, your grief journey is just that—yours. While you may experience the same loss as someone else and your emotions and reactions may even parallel others, your actual grieving process will be as unique as you are. The GRACE Grief Model affirms this individualization of the grieving process and will help you understand and work through your losses in a way that supports your unique needs and maps your unique grief plan.

SYMPTOMS OF GRIEF

Symptoms of grief can be broad and vary from person to person. However, general grief symptoms most often include profound sadness, somatization (physical symptoms), disbelief, and longing.[4] In cases of death, the bereaved person's grief symptoms can even involve seeing or hearing the dead loved one.[5] Initially, these symptoms can overtake us and even consume us, but over time, grief symptoms generally subside.[6] It is normal and, yes, even healthy for feelings of grief to follow loss. However, it is important that we recognize potential grief complications, such as severe grief feelings or prolonged grief feelings, which can require professional support.

---

[4] Shear, 2011; Thimm & Holland, 2017

[5] Shear, 2011; Thimm & Holland, 2017

[6] Thimm & Holland, 2017

EMOTIONS VS. FEELINGS

Within this book, I often use the terms "feelings" and "emotions" inter-changeably because this is how most people understand and speak of them, yet I acknowledge that there are important differences between the two expressions. According to the neuroscience work of Antonio Damasio and Gil Carvalho,[7] emotions are observable, unconscious behaviors, whereas feelings are the subjective experience of emotion. Emotions are physical signals within the body occurring in response to an external stimulus. Feelings are mental experiences of the body[8] that occur as our brain attempts to make sense of emotions. Said another way, "(e)motions play out in the theater of the body. Feelings play out in the theater of the mind."[9] Examples of emotions include fear, anger, sadness, joy, etc. Feelings are how we consciously express those emotions. Whereas feelings are experienced consciously. Emotions can be experienced either consciously or subconsciously. Simply put, emotions are physical, and feelings are mental.[10]

The grief process begins with a perceived loss event, which then impacts our body at a biological physical level (emotion), and next affects us mentally (feeling).

Figure 1

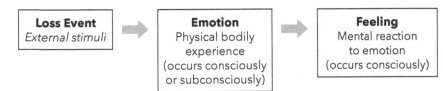

---

[7] Carvalho, 2013

[8] Damasio & Carvalho, 2013

[9] Damasio, 1999, p. 28

[10] Bitbrain, 2019

GRIEF IS AN EMOTION, FIRST AND FOREMOST

The notion of grief as first an emotion is evidenced by both an understanding that emotion precedes feeling and emotions are the foundations for feelings, and also through an understanding of the brain's anatomical and biochemical pathways. There are many parts of the brain involved in emotion, including four structures that play a primary role: the hypothalamus (executor of emotion, helps relay messages), the amygdala (orchestrates emotion), the striatum (supports formation of habits, interacts with the prefrontal cortex), and the prefrontal cortex (evaluates whether an emotional response is appropriate or not).[11] The amygdala, which connects the unconscious and conscious aspects of how we experience emotion, links to the prefrontal cortex (the brain's "logic center"). The prefrontal cortex is responsible for regulating feelings, the conscious expression of emotions.[12] All emotions we experience result from our brain structures responding to the amygdala and acting on its direction.

We are learning that emotions are biological and not mere philosophical matters limited to introspective measures as once believed until the 20th century.[13] Advances in science point to emotions as biological reactions[14] that can be examined and understood in evidential ways, including advanced brain imaging, brain mapping, and direct testing measures. Quite simply, emotions are no longer regarded as conjured up reactions or over-reactions, and no longer are they relegated to science speculation. Rather, emotions are now viewed as an intricate chemical and anatomical biological response of our bodily system necessary not only for our health, but also for our survival.

---

[11] Kandel, 2018

[12] Kandel, 2018

[13] Okon-Singer, Hendler, Pessoa, & Shackman, 2015

[14] Gross, 2013

While thoughts, for example, can trigger an emotional response, emerging understanding of the body and brain's biological pathways and processes suggest that even our thoughts are first an emotion. Thoughts stem from the "emotional center" of our brain (the amygdala) in reaction to external stimuli entering our brain, which then follows a pathway that first passes through the amygdala before traveling to the "logic center" of our brain (the prefrontal cortex). Hence, our thoughts are first emotions whether we recognize the emotion or not. This pathway even aligns with how the brain physically grows, since the amygdala develops earlier than the prefrontal cortex.[15]

Calvin's "Bad" Boss

Calvin came to counseling to address relationship issues he was having at work with his boss. Calvin said, "I knew in my gut this guy was bad when I first began working for him." However, the more Calvin explored this situation in counseling, he eventually was able to recognize that his initial "gut" feelings were actually his emotions. It seemed Calvin's boss strongly triggered Clavin in that the boss subconsciously reminded Calvin of a boy who frequently bullied him during middle school. Calvin's amygdala (emotion center) was signaling an alarm for Calvin to beware of this boss based on prior feelings (anger, hurt, etc.) attached to another person from long ago. These feelings then resulted in Calvin's thoughts (from the prefrontal cortex) that his current boss was "bad." Understanding how his emotions were influencing his thoughts helped Calvin be aware of his biased judgments about his boss and allowed Calvin to begin grieving the painful experience of being bullied as a youth.

---

[15]   Tottenham & Gabard-Durnam, 2017

There remains still much to learn and understand about emotions. Some modern scholars suggest emotions are likely more closely linked to our thoughts than once suspected. Historically, scholars have tended to treat emotions and thoughts as different.[16] However, based on neuroimaging, a more contemporary understanding disputes firm demarcation and suggests there exists a greater integration between emotion and thought than once was believed.[17] These findings point towards the interweaving of brain processes and functions in ways we are only now just beginning to understand.

GRIEF TYPES

As we learn about grief, it is helpful to recognize there are many different types of grief. The six types we will discuss are normal grief, prolonged grief, anticipatory grief, disenfranchised grief, abstract grief, and ambiguous grief. It is noteworthy to mention that grief types can be overlapping. For example, the nature of ambiguous grief (ongoing loss that lacks closure) can often result in accompanying disenfranchised grief (unsupported and minimized loss).

Normal Grief (Integrated Grief)

Normal grief is healthy and part of the common human condition. Normal grief differs from abnormal (prolonged or complicated) grief in that "normal grief progresses from acute to integrated grief."[18] Importantly, "normal" does not refer to a timeline, as there is no normal timeframe for grief, but rather this describes a type of grief progression. Normal progression entails moving from an acute state, marked by mental and

---

[16] Schmitter, 2014

[17] Lindquist and Barrett, 2012; Barrett and Satpute, 2013; Pessoa, 2013; Raz et al., 2014

[18] Moayedoddin & Markowitz, 2015, p. 364

emotional anguish, repeated thoughts of the loss, and neglect of routine life functioning, towards a healthy integration of grief signaled by acceptance of the loss, a reduction in mental and emotional suffering, and a return to a normalized life. Acute grief refers to grief occurring during the initial phase after a loss. Acute grief overshadows a person's life and is marked by yearning, sadness, longing, along with anxiety, anger, bitterness, guilt and/or shame.[19] Normal or integrated grief occurs when a person adapts to the loss. This adaptation does not signal the end of grief but rather indicates grief has found a healthy place in the rhythm of their life.

Prolonged Grief (Complicated Grief)

What happens when the natural normal flow of the grief process is disrupted? Interference in a healthy grieving process could herald the onset of prolonged grief. While the majority of people's grief response will be "normal" and move them out of woundedness into a place of healthy healing after a loss event, for some the reaction to loss can be abnormal. Abnormal reactions of grief or complicated grief result from an obstruction of the path to integrated grief, causing profound and incessant distress pertaining to the loss.[20] Prolonged grief is an unhealthy grief response involving bereavement, requiring diagnosis by a mental health professional. A diagnosis of prolonged grief is based on grief severity and duration and, if not treated, can cause long-term psychological problems. Prolonged grief signals the normal process of healing has been derailed.[21] Statistics indicate the approximate number of persons struggling with

---

[19]   Center for Prolonged Grief, 2023

[20]   Shear, 2011; Simon, 2013

[21]   Shear, 2011

complicated grief is at least 7 percent in bereaved populations and 4 percent in general populations.[22]

If not treated, prolonged grief is a general health hazard[23] and viewed as a potentially life-threating condition.[24] Persons with prolonged grief are at increased risk for co-existing mental and physical conditions, which includes higher risk of death, cancer, cardiovascular trouble, high blood pressure, suicidality, eating problems/disorders,[25] and depression.[26] Post-Traumatic Stress Disorder (PTSD) is also understood as a side effect of prolonged grief.[27] Prolonged grief symptoms include rumination, inability to make sense of the loss, catastrophic thinking, and avoidance, and is associated with prolonged distress, suicidality, and negative health.[28]

As previously discussed in this text, there is a distinction between ongoing adaptive grief work, which is healthy, and grief that is prolonged, which is unhealthy. The GRACE Grief Model supports healthy ongoing grief work while drawing attention and awareness to unhealthy grieving, including prolonged grief.

Anticipatory Grief

Another common type of grief response is anticipatory grief, which is understood as grief that occurs prior to a loss, as distinguished from

---

[22] Enez, 2018; Kersting, Brahler, Glaesmer, & Wagner, 2011; Rosner, Pfoh, & Kotoucova, 2011

[23] Miyabayashi & Yasuda, 2007; Nakajima, 2018

[24] Shear et al., 2011

[25] Ito et al., 2012

[26] Simon, 2013

[27] Linde, Treml, Steinig, Nagl, & Kersting, 2017

[28] Shear, 2011

grief occurring at or after a loss.[29] How can you have grief over a loss that has not happened? This type of grief can actually be fairly common and occurs when we believe correctly or incorrectly that a loss is likely to occur or is going to occur. Examples include concerns that a company's cost-reductions will result in layoffs, escalation of fighting and hurt feelings between couples causing one partner to assume the relationship is ending, or seeing grandmother's illness progress and sensing she may not live much longer.

Disenfranchised Grief

In some cases, grief feels as if it cannot be openly or publicly acknowledged, socially supported, or publicly mourned, which is referred to as disenfranchised grief.[30] These types of losses are largely unsupported. When I worked caring for the elderly in one of my church roles, I often heard these types of losses referred to as "non-casserole" events, meaning the parishioners and others never or rarely brought meals or other offers of support to those struggling with disenfranchised grief. Common examples of disenfranchised grief include LGBTQ+ issues, pregnancy losses, disabilities, affairs, estrangements, pet losses, etc.

Grief Caused by Abstract Loss

We universally recognize that loss includes physical losses, like the loss of people, animals, and things. These types of losses are tangible and more easily understood by most. However, not every loss is tangible or easily understood. Loss can also include the abstract, such as loss of one's beliefs, loss of love, loss of dreams and hopes, loss of independence, loss of ideations, etc. These types of non-tangible losses are abstract loss.

---

[29] Hamilton, 2016

[30] Doka, 1989; Lathrop, 2017

Ambiguous Grief

Ambiguous losses are losses that have no closure. These involve "a situation of unclear loss that remains unverified and thus without resolution."[31]Ambiguous losses may go unrecognized, which can result in disenfranchisement. Ambiguous losses refer to the physical or psychological experiences that are not concrete.[32] Examples of physical ambiguous loss includes missing persons, kidnappings, a person presumed dead but whose body was never found, incarcerations, missing pets, etc. Psychological examples of ambiguous loss include chronic mental or physical illness, such as when you or a loved one has dementia, traumatic brain injury, etc. The ambiguous loss cycle is never ending and rarely closes, resulting in a prolonged loss experience.[33]

GRIEF'S IMPACT

Grief, as we have been learning, can impact us in many ways. So far, we have seen that grief affects us physically and mentally and we know grief's impacts can be felt individually and collectively. Grief's effects on us can also include the following:

Avoidant behaviors. Actions you may take to escape from difficult thoughts and feelings. Sometimes we avoid by what we do (e.g., overwork instead of dealing with our painful feelings of loss) or what we do not do (e.g., avoid driving by the road where the death of a loved one occurred). An avoidant grief style is frequently an attempt to prevent

---

[31] Boss, 2016, p. 270

[32] Betz & Thorngren, 2006

[33] Betz & Thorngren, 2006

thinking about a loss, however avoidant behaviors often result in the opposite effect.[34]

Somatization. The body can express psychological distress in the form of physical symptoms, which is referred to as somatization. People can mistake these symptoms as a physical problem for which they seek medical help. In cases of somatization, common complaints include body pain, fatigue, and perceived cardiac or gastrointestinal issues. This can even be accompanied by, for example, palpitations, dizziness, diarrhea, and limb weakness. For those who are somatic, these bodily complaints are not the result of physiological problems, but rather manifest from psychological issues, like depression or anxiety.[35] In these cases, the bodily distress, while not of physical origin, is very real and not imagined or made up. Most of us will experience some form of somatization at some time, such as getting a headache after an intensely stressful day.

Hyperarousal. Hyperarousal involves a 24-hour state of elevated cognitive and physiological activation, and often is associated with insomnia.[36]

Eating issues. Grief can affect our eating. Sometimes we may eat too much or too little. For example, eating alone (perhaps because of divorce or if a spouse has died) is a risk factor for nutritional vulnerability in later life.[37]

---

[34] Schneck et al., 2019

[35] Henningsen, 2018

[36] Altena et al., 2017

[37] Vesnaver, Keller, Sutherland, Maitland, & Locher, 2016

Panic attacks. Panic is overwhelming fright, fear, or terror, and it can happen to any person and, at times, can even make you feel as though you are having a heart attack or that you are dying.[38] Typically, a panic attack comes without warning, but most, fortunately, are short-lived. However, if panic is frequent and followed by at least 30 days of worrying that you may have another panic attack, this can be panic disorder.[39]

---

[38] Torpy, Burke, & Golub, 2011
[39] Torpy, Burke, & Golub, 2011

Chapter 2

THE GRACE GRIEF MODEL: AN OVERVIEW

THE GRACE GRIEF MODEL

The word "grace" refers to receiving an undeserved or unmerited favor. It is getting something, a gift, which is given without having to earn it. The gift of grace is given freely by the giver, but for the gift to be given, the recipient must do something: grace must be *received*. We, as the recipient, must choose to receive the gift. The concept of grace is fitting for the GRACE Grief Model in that grieving is an innate process for healing given freely to us, as this is hardwired into our very DNA (as I detail later in this book). Our responsibility is to receive the gift of grace, which is a gift of healing. As we will explore, the GRACE Grief Model helps you understand the gifts grieving brings and invites you to accept these gifts of recovery.

ABOUT THE GRACE GRIEF MODEL

The GRACE Grief Model is a new grief model that supports healthy healing from loss. The GRACE model provides hope for those who have been stalled or stuck in their grief journey. This model highlights a way forward by offering new approaches to work through loss, and by providing an expanded understanding of grief as biologically imperative, emotionally healing, and spiritually nurturing.

The GRACE Grief Model offers five steps toward healing:

> **Step 1:** G – Grief redefined as **G**ood, **G**oing to ebb and flow, and ultimately a **G**ift

> **Step 2:** R – **R**e-story the loss narrative

> **Step 3:** A – **A**dopt new healthy ways to grieve

> **Step 4:** C – **C**onnect with self and others

> **Step 5:** E – **E**ngage in a new normal within a livable pattern of grief work

WHAT DOES THIS MEAN?

The GRACE Grief Model (also referred to in this text as the GRACE model or simply GRACE) affirms healthy grieving and offers a powerful evidenced-based opportunity to heal and grow through loss recovery and restoration, including constructing meaning from loss as we move forward in the grief process. The GRACE model meets you wherever you are in your grief journey and provides a map towards healing wholeness. This model offers an integration of cognitive behavioral therapy (CBT) and narrative therapy elements within a framework that supports individual beliefs, goals, and sense of purpose (meaning making). The goal of this approach is to foster effective healing through an evidenced-based approach aimed at treating those struggling with grief, including prolonged grief.

In the GRACE Grief Model, CBT and narrative therapy elements within a meaning making framework were selected and incorporated for several reasons:

- **First, the CBT techniques**, in general, target the loss-related processes and focus on symptoms of painful intrusive memories and behavioral avoidance.

- **Second, narrative therapy (NT) techniques** can help explore multidimensional identities and also remove the identity as "the problem" from persons struggling with loss. Narrative therapy also supports the telling and re-telling of the loss story in ways that promote healing. (Of note, for those diagnosed with prolonged grief disorder, an additional form of narrative support, such as narrative reconstructive (NR) offering a more intense and directed narrative structure and process than traditional NT may be added by the mental healthcare professional. More on this later in the chapter.)

- **Third, meaning making elements** support the overall restoration by helping re-establish connection with valued life goals, including one's own spirituality. In this text, meaning making will be explored primarily through the context of spirituality. Spiritualty can impact one's understanding of grief as well as provide coping resources in dealing with loss.[40] The term "spirituality" used in the GRACE Grief Model, as well as for the purpose of this book, follows Rosmarin's[41] understanding that spirituality is any way of relating to that which is sacred or to a greater reality, and views religion as a subset of the spiritual involving culturally bound or institutional ways of relating to the sacred.

---

[40] Wortman & Park, 2008

[41] Rosmarin, 2018

WHY THE GRACE GRIEF MODEL WAS CREATED

Grief affects every person at some point in their life. For most, grief's impact is normative, and people are able to recover and move forward with their life; however, for some, the grief experience can become dire and impede life functioning. I developed the GRACE Grief Model to help address a problem. As an ordained United Methodist minister (order of deacon) and Licensed Professional Counselor, my work has often centered on supporting those struggling with loss. During my training at The Menninger Clinic in Houston, Texas, I was mentored by Rev. Salvador Delmundo Jr. While at Menniger, I created and lead an in-patient grief group, which furthered my focus and interest in the area of grief and loss. During this time, I was also introduced to new models of care, including the bio-psycho-social-spiritual model, which I later incorporated into the GRACE Grief Model (I note here that, while the term bio-psycho-social-spiritual typically is not written with each word hyphenated, I elect to do so in my work to emphasize each component). During these years, I also had the opportunity to visit many times with the late Dr. Coleen O'Byrne, who was then a staff psychologist at Menninger. My conversations with Dr. O'Byrne about emotions and feelings helped pave the way towards my development of the GRACE Grief Model's 3 Steps for Processing Feelings (discussed in later chapters).

As I continued to work with people in their personal grief journeys, I routinely found myself searching unsuccessfully for an existing grief model that integrated cognitive behavior therapy (CBT) and narrative therapy utilizing meaning making inclusive of spirituality. Because I was never able to find this model, I created it. I began the conceptual outline of this model during my time at Menninger, researched its foundation and formulated the major precepts during my doctoral work, and later finalized the creation of the GRACE Grief Model during my ministry of professional counseling. The goal of this model is to offer an alternative grief treatment aimed at facilitating the grieving process and expanding grief treatment options to help more people, inclusive of at-risk populations.

HOW THE GRACE GRIEF MODEL WAS CREATED

As stated, two of the psychotherapy models integrated into the GRACE Grief Model are cognitive behavioral therapy (CBT) and narrative therapy. CBT has long been deemed effective for the treatment of grief, including complicated grief.[42] The overarching goal of CBT is to introduce and utilize a variety of cognitive, behavioral, and emotion-focused techniques targeted at changing maladaptive cognitions.[43] Yet, I found that even this evidenced-based model often fell short as an effective stand-alone grief therapy (my reasons and findings on this have been detailed in the Introduction section of this book). In short, CBT does not seem to help many patients feel their emotions or connect to their past pain experiences for the purpose of processing and learning. CBT also lacks cultural and ethical consideration, including pluralistic identities. Further, CBT requires the patient to move towards logical and rational thought, which can be difficult for those grieving. Finally, CBT alone does not seem to help patients recognize "the problem" apart from themselves. Addressing these types of struggles is where I found incorporating narrative therapy and meaning making (including spirituality) into CBT immensely helpful for my patients.

Narrative therapy is a form of psychotherapy which conceptualizes that people are separate from the problems, wherein problems are viewed

---

[42] CG; Boelen & de Keijser, 2007

[43] Hofmann, Asnaani, Vonk, Sawyer, & Fang, 2012

as narrow and limiting client stories that do not align with the preferred experiences of self.[44] Narrative therapy aims to support re-authoring stories through core processes that include the deconstruction of problem-saturated stories, externalization of the story separating the person from the problem, mapping the effects of the problems, and re-authoring and creating a preferred narrative that offers unique outcomes and produces supportive networks.[45] In full disclosure, while narrative therapy currently lacks the broad body of research and systematic review needed to affirm it as evidenced-based, narrative therapy has for decades been demonstrated to have "practice-based evidence."[46]

In addition to narrative therapy, narrative reconstruction may also be used with patients diagnosed with prolonged grief disorder. While both narrative therapy and narrative reconstruction are rooted in the storying and re-storying process, narrative reconstruction offers those battling prolonged grief a potentially promising evidenced-based way to process grief through a systematic reconstruction of their loss narrative along chronological timelines.[47] Narrative reconstruction requires the patient and therapist to work closely together and should be done within the therapeutic setting with a psychotherapist present. Initially used to treat post-traumatic stress disorder (PTSD) patients, narrative reconstruction has recently been demonstrated useful with those struggling from prolonged grief disorder.[48] However, for those not diagnosed with prolonged grief, narrative therapy seems to offer a more optimal therapy choice for several reasons, including narrative therapy does not necessarily require a psychotherapist to be present and narrative therapy allows for a more

---

[44] White & Epston, 1990; Williams-Reade, Freitas, & Lawson, 2014

[45] White & Epston, 1990; Williams-Reade, Freitas, & Lawson, 2014

[46] Epston, 1992

[47] Elinger, Hasson-Ohayon, Bar-Shachar, Peri, 2023

[48] Elinger, Hasson-Ohayon, Bar-Shachar, Peri, 2023

flexible adaptive use of narrative for healing. For these reasons, narrative therapy will be the narrative-based therapy focus within this work.

The third model used in the development of the GRACE model addresses meaning making. Meaning making has attracted scholars over the centuries and remains "the central issue of human existence."[49] It has traditionally been understood to involve coming to see a situation in a different way and reconsidering one's beliefs and goals in order to regain consistency among them.[50] Dr. Crystal Park's approach to meaning making builds on existing understandings of global meaning and incorporates global meaning (beliefs about the universe and one's role it it) with situational meaning (meanings based on events from one's own environment).[51]

Park's Meaning Making Model[52] offers the specific meaning making model which I adapted and integrated into the GRACE model. Park's model offers a framework of meaning making that provides an overview of popular research and theory on the matters of meaning, spirituality, and stress-related growth.[53] Park's model supports spiritualty and supports the concept that spirituality can impact ones understanding of grief, as well as provide coping resources and meaning in dealing with loss.[54]

Humankind's "need for meaning" can be understood as the "need for a functional meaning system."[55] Finding or creating meaning is a core human motive which addresses meaning-related needs: agency, control,

---

[49] Park, 2017, p.15

[50] Davis, Wortman, Lehman, & Silver, 2000

[51] Park, 2017

[52] MMM; Park, 2013

[53] Park, 2013

[54] Wortmann & Park, 2008

[55] Park, Edmondson, & Hale-Smith, 2013; Park, 2020, p. 273

certainty, identity, social validation, values, and mortality defense.[56] According to Park,[57] one's comprehensibility, purpose, and subjective sense of meaning informs one's cognitive, motivational, and emotional aspects of experiences. Thereby, when our personal meaning system is working well, the world and our identity in the world makes sense creating for us peace and purpose; however, when our meaning system is not working well, the world and who we are in the world lacks purpose and clarity, creating distress.[58]

FILLING A GAP THROUGH CONGRUENT FIT

CBT + NT + MM = G.R.A.C.E.

Blending CBT and narrative therapy (NT) within a meaning making (MM) framework, inclusive of spirituality, provides key elements missing from other grief models. Each of the core foundational components of the GRACE Grief Model (CBT, NT, and meaning making) have demonstrated efficacies in treating grief and offer congruent and complimentary elements. Combined, these parts augment and balance one another well and present a singular model, the GRACE Grief Model, supporting a new way to address grief that fills known gaps.

HOW THE MODEL CAN HELP: A GRACE-FULL SOLUTION

The struggle with grief is two-fold: people struggle not only from losses, but also because they do not know how to engage in healthy grief work to address those losses. Many have neither been allowed to follow their

---

[56]   Park, 2017

[57]   Park, 2017

[58]   Park, 2017

innate grief instincts nor taught to grieve in healthy ways necessary to move forward in the grieving process. The GRACE model offers a new way to grieve and progress through loss, helping those stuck in grief to learn and practice healthier adaptive ways to move forward.

The GRACE Grief Model offers a solution of hope and healing by:

- Promoting loss recovery and restoration
- Encouraging healthy grieving processes
- Supporting a person's unique grief journey and individuality
- Encouraging inclusion of meaning making, including one's personal spirituality, in the grieving process.

THE GRACE GRIEF MAP

The GRACE Grief Model uses the meaning making framework to create a "map" to guide us forward in the grief process. Again, meaning making centers on beliefs, goals, and sense of purpose, and involves understanding a situation differently and being able to reexamine your beliefs and goals in effort to reach consistency among them. The GRACE Grief Model Grief Map (or GRACE Grief Map, for short) was constructed using Park's Meaning Making Model with elements of Hill's[59] meaning making processes.

To begin, it is important to state that, although the map demonstrates linear movement, we must keep in mind the grief process is not necessarily linear. Everyone's grief is personal and may progress (or digress) in different ways and at different times. Looking at the GRACE Grief Map, we find that when our beliefs, goals, and sense of purpose (World View) do not align with the meanings we have given to a specific loss (Loss View), this can create an unhealthy meaning of the loss, derailing

---

[59] Hill, 2018

our healthy grieving process. When this occurs, there are steps forward through which we can move to support our journey from "unhealthy" meaning making to "healthy" meaning making.

The steps forward include these actions:

- **Pausing, stopping, and reflecting.** Taking time out to orient yourself as to where you are regarding your grief (e.g., how you are doing, what you are doing, how you feel, etc.) can provide you essential time and evaluative information that can then support healthy forward progress through your grief journey.

- **Creating a sense of meaning** (includes meaning, mattering or significance, purpose, coherence, and reflectivity) that supports healthy beliefs, goals, and sense of purpose. This can be achieved through deliberate intent and exercises done during the time one takes to pause, stop, and reflect during the grief journey. Again, meaning making in this work incorporates each person's own spirituality.

The primary purpose of the GRACE Grief Map is to bring awareness of how our perceptions and views impact healthy and unhealthy grief processes. Also, for those stuck in unhealthy grieving, the GRACE Grief Map provides a stepwise process for moving forward towards healing and wholeness.

GRACE Grief Model: Grief Map*

1. Define World View
Your World View is your general beliefs, goals, sense of purpose.

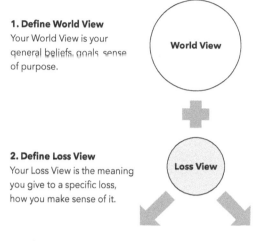

2. Define Loss View
Your Loss View is the meaning you give to a specific loss, how you make sense of it.

3. Unhealthy Meaning (Misalignment)
Unhealthy meaning making creates unhealthy grieving. This results when your World View is *not* in alignment with your Loss View.

Healthy Meaning (Alignment)
Healthy meaning making creates healthy grieving. This results when your World View is in alignment with your Loss View.

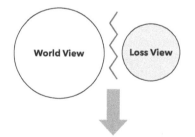

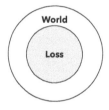

HOW TO MOVE TOWARDS HEALTHY MEANING MAKING

4. Stop, Pause & Reflect
Stop, pause, and reflect on loss and where you are in the grieving process.

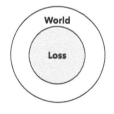

5. Search & Construct
Find meaning and create new understanding of loss.

6. Healthy Meaning (Alignment)

Figure 2.

* The GRACE Grief Model™ Grief Map includes adaptations from Park (2013) and Hill (2018)

Chapter 3

STEP 1: GRIEF, REDEFINED

"Part of every misery is…the misery's shadow or reflection: the fact that you don't merely suffer but have to keep on thinking about the fact that you suffer. I not only live each endless day in grief but live each day thinking about living each day in grief."

—C.S. Lewis

A NEW UNDERSTANDING OF GRIEF

The mere concept of grief, for many, is fraught with ideations of pain and suffering. When facilitating grief groups and conducting individual counseling sessions, I often invite clients to describe their understanding of grief. The words I most frequently hear used to depict grief include sadness, loss, anger, hopelessness, guilt, overwhelmed, fear, loneliness, and pain. While these can definitely be part of grief, these descriptors alone do not come close to encompassing the fullness of what grief really is. From my grief work with others, as well as my own experience with loss, I have grown to understand that grief is about so much more than the feelings of hurt people most frequently associate with it; grief at its core is about healing and moving one through the pain to a place understanding and peace—a place of *shalom*.

The emotions of loss, including pain and suffering, are part of our human condition. Everybody hurts from loss at some time. Buddhists acknowledge this suffering through their teachings of the Four Noble Truths: 1. The truth of suffering, 2. The truth of the cause of suffering, 3. The truth of the end of suffering, and 4. The truth of the path that leads to the end of suffering. Christians also are taught in scripture that pain and sorrow will be part of everyday life (John 16:33; Acts 14:22). There is a process we must travel when moving from pain and suffering into a place of hope and peace. The GRACE Grief Model offers this process. In the GRACE model, grief, including all its sorrow, is understood as a remarkable process inviting opportunity for healing in which grief is understood as biologically imperative, emotional healing, and spiritually nurturing.

GRIEF REDEFINED

What is grief, really? In the GRACE Grief Model, grief is redefined as follows:

- Grief is **good**
- Grief is **going to ebb and flow** (it is cyclical)
- Grief is ultimately a **gift**

When understood as *good, going to ebb and flow (cyclical)*, and a *gift*, grief can provide a way of helping you progress through difficult emotions, such as pain and suffering, and move towards healing and a hopeful future story. In the upcoming chapters, you will learn why grief is indeed good, explore the cyclical nature of grief and learn to anticipate and accept grief's approach, and open yourself to regard grief as a gift to be invited into your life.

GRIEF IS GOOD

Waves of loss ebb and flow throughout our lives, but within these murky waters, hope floats.

In each new wave of grief, we find opportunity to heal. In our sorrow, we are presented a chance to feel, to name, and to learn from our wounded places. Among the brokenness, we can find the gift grieving brings—the opening to move from pain to peace, from heartbreak to hope.

The emotions of grief can be extremely difficult, but essential to our growth, restoration, and healing. Grief is, in fact, good. Yet grief certainly does not feel good, so how is grief good? Grief is good because, if we grieve in healthy ways, **grief is how we heal from loss.**

WE ARE HARD-WIRED TO HEAL FROM LOSS

You were wonderfully made. Every person has been formed out of flesh and bones, and also out of stardust.[60] Our bodies are each made up of atoms that are billions of years old.[61] Each body is hard-wired with insight and intuition that is formed from our very DNA. The body has innate wisdom, and that innate wisdom includes mechanisms to help us heal.

When our bodies are injured, they attempt to heal themselves, much like the scab that forms to heal a skinned knee or the bones that knit themselves back together after a break. While at times we may need support for our healing processes, the body is still amazingly adept at trying to mend itself. This innate healing process includes our body's attempt to recover from losses. Losses are a natural and inevitable part of every life, like a thread that weaves in and out of the fabric of our life's narrative. The body is remarkably created to heal from losses through an innate process, and we call this process grieving.

---

[60] Schrijver & Schrijver, 2015

[61] Schrijver & Schrijver, 2015

Sea Glass: A Metaphor for the Grief Process

Several years ago, I happened across an elegantly simple yet powerful way of understanding the grief process as explained by author and bereavement counselor, Ellen Frankel. I was able to personally share with Frankel my appreciation of her story and, specifically, her sea glass analogy which she graciously granted me permission to share. The following is Frankel's story, which includes a comparison of the grieving process to the rather remarkable and, yes, arduous process in which sea glass is formed.

When you break a glass on the kitchen floor, you have to be careful when you go to clean up. The glass is sharp—so very sharp—so as you pick it up, piece by piece, you have to go slowly, touch the glass cautiously, because even the slightest encounter with the edge can pierce your skin and you hurt, and you bleed. The shards of glass are harsh, and the edges cut deeply.

Now imagine that those broken pieces of glass have been thrown into the ocean. They are at the mercy of the current and have to let go into the forces of nature. Some days the ocean roars with big forceful waves and the glass is tossed and churned and thrown along with the rocks and sand. Other times the ocean is gentle, and the glass is stroked by the rhythm of the tide. Yet just as the gentle ocean lulls the glass with its soothing melody, another storm hits and the glass is once again pushed against the force of currents, the force of the moon and the heavens. And yet again, at some point the ocean quiets, the flow is once again soft, the waves flow like the inhalation and exhalation of the breath, arriving at the shore, hugging the sand.

And at some point, there you are, on a warm, sunny July day, walking along the seashore when you stop because just in front of you, sitting amidst pebbles and rocks and periwinkle shells, is a piece of sea glass. You bend down to pick it up, marveling at your good fortune to find this treasure. Holding it in your hands you feel its smoothness and the places where the sea glass might have a slight ridge. You can rub it on all of its sides, for no longer are there sharp edges. Instead, the edges have become solid and smooth, and you can hold it tightly in your hand without fear of injury. In fact, holding it in your hand feels fortifying and strengthening. We actively seek these brilliant pieces of sea glass precisely because they echo the beauty of survival, of resiliency, and of hope. With tenderness and love you are able to hold this piece of sea glass and learn its unique features. Where once the edges of the glass were jagged and sharp, now the edges are ever softly rounded, so that you can run a finger over them repeatedly, and it will not take your blood. That is how grief can change...Those are the edges of grief.

GRIEF: FROM MISALIGNMENT TO ALIGNMENT

As the GRACE Grief Model's Grief Map illustrates, a primary goal necessary to move forward in the grieving process includes moving from misalignment to alignment with World View and Loss View. As you proceed through the GRACE Grief Map, you can facilitate understanding of these critical steps towards healing:

Level 1: Awareness. Awareness means knowing your current World View and Loss View. This can require some time and deliberation on your part to examine and understand how your World View might be in misalignment with your Loss View. Awareness also includes an understanding of what possible unhealthy meanings you are making because of any misalignment between the World View and Loss View.

Level 2: Action. Grieving in healthy ways takes work, which is why we refer to this as "grief work." The work of grief involves stopping, pausing, reflecting, and developing and deepening a sense of meaning, mattering, purpose, coherence, and reflectivity.

Level 3: Change. When healthy World Views and Loss Views are in alignment, this results in healthy meanings made about loss.

The following offers a demonstration of what World View and Loss View can look like as perceived by a person struggling from the death of a loved one. In this example, we follow the developing views of a bereaved parent, Margaret, after the death of their child as Margaret moves from misalignment to alignment.

Margaret, a Bereaved Parent: Example of Misalignment

Worldview: I believe bad things should not happen to good people. I believe suffering comes from something evil. I believe in God and know that God is good. As long as I am faithful, I believe God will always keep evil and suffering from my life.

Loss View: My daughter is dead, but this cannot be true because we are a faithful family and God was supposed to prevent this evil. Also, parents are supposed to die before their children.

Unhealthy Meaning Made: My daughter's death was meaningless and should never have happened because we are faithful. God did not stop her death and I'm just so very deeply sad and angry! I'm mad at God!

Margaret, a Bereaved Parent: Example of Alignment

Worldview: I believe bad things happen to good people. I believe there is a difference between evil and suffering. I know that all evil causes suffering, but I believe suffering is not always the result of evil. Sometimes suffering happens because of other things, like natural laws of the universe that can set into motion events that can result in catastrophe without evil being involved. Or a person's free will can have unintended negative impacts that can result in suffering, but that doesn't mean evil is involved. I believe in God and know that God is good. I believe God is with us and grieves in our suffering.

Loss View: Parents typically die before their children, but this is, sadly, not always the case. People do not always die when they are old. Many times, it is the young who die far too soon, like my daughter.

Healthy Meaning Made: When my daughter died, I was so sad and I saw everything at that time through the lens of anger. For a long time, I was mad at everything and everyone, even God. I felt like it was God who allowed her death to happen, taking her away from me. But in time, I came to understand that God did not cause my daughter to die. Even though I don't know why God didn't perform a miracle and save my daughter, I no longer blame God. Eventually, I grew to appreciate all that God did for my daughter and also for me. I realize now it was God who brought many helpers into our lives who offered comfort, support, and love in the darkest of days. I'm still very sad about my daughter's death, but the pain is no longer as deep. I can finally think about her and talk about her, recalling fond memories and smiling about the beauty of her life and not solely focused on the tragedy of her untimely death.

Ryan & Sam

Years ago, my son Ryan was working on his elementary school homework. The assignment was to describe both his worst day and his best day. Ryan began by detailing his worst day—it was the day our dog Sam died. Sam, a large affable yellow lab, had been part of the family since before Ryan's birth, so there was not a time that Ryan's memories did not include his beloved dog. Ryan wrote about how he leaned to walk by holding onto Sam and how he spent hours in the backyard hunting with Sam and digging up buried treasures in the sandbox. Ryan also listed details of Sam's rapidly declining health and the constant pain Sam's tortured body now endured. Ryan spoke of the difficult acknowledgement when it was ultimately time to have Sam put down. He then described that very long day, the day of Sam's death, expressing the deep sadness he felt.

Next, Ryan moved to the second homework prompt and described his best day. Surprisingly and perhaps even shockingly, he spoke of the same day—the day Sam died. How could this also be one of Ryan's best days? For Ryan, the loss of Sam and the immense pain of that day was very real and very difficult. However, in his memory of the day, Ryan also incorporated the deep appreciation and love he felt for Sam. Ryan, even as a child in grief, believed it was his privilege to be with Sam at the end. Ryan felt a sense of duty and was grateful to be there when Sam needed him, even at the very difficult moment of Sam's passing, especially since Sam had always been there for Ryan.

> Ryan's world view included the understanding that someday his dog would die. When that day came, he then created a loss view that regarded being present on Sam's death day as difficult, but an honor. Ryan believed he helped Sam depart this world while also helping to provide himself an opportunity to say good-bye to his much-loved pet. In this case, Ryan's loss view aligned with his world view, resulting in healthy alignment and healing meanings made from the loss event.

GRIEF IS GOING TO EBB AND FLOW

Grief comes and goes like a wave; it is cyclical. Physics teaches us waves are disturbances that travel through space and transfer energy from one place to another. Just as water's energy can be collected and transferred into a process that yields electricity, the collective energy within our emotional grief waves can be harnessed and transferred into our healing plan, our healing process, as we direct the energy embedded in feelings towards healing.

Grief does not occur according to rules or necessarily in stages, rather grief occurs on a continuum. Grief is cyclical, it ebbs and flows back and forth, in a continual wave-like rhythm inviting the healing process. Losses—big and small—are part of our normal human condition and every person will experience some type of loss; the longer we live, the more loss we likely will encounter. The feelings and emotions associated with loss are understood as grief. It is within this beautiful ongoing processing of grief that we are invited into the powerful healing process.

Grief remains a constant part of human life. Our charge and our challenge is to grow and heal *with* grief, using the energy of grief to propel us forward. Rather than fighting against the waves, we can use that energy the waves produce. How can we allow grief in and harness those waves? To begin, instead of relegating grief to a set of actions on a checklist or phases we must endure and move through quickly, recognizing that grief is the underrated harbinger of healing that begs (at times demands) our attention and even may require a seat at the table.

Grief is not a single storm that blows into our life, but rather grief is more like the weather itself—sometimes calm and sometimes turbulent, but always present. Ocean waves are predominantly created by weather, specifically winds moving across the water's surface. Winds of loss will always move across life's surfaces. As with the weather, grief impacts us continually and is itself necessary for our human existence. The key is to remember that grief is good, grief will forever be part of the rhythm of our lives, and we should learn to direct and accept its energy as healing properties.

GRIEF IS A GIFT

Loss can be devastating and cause great pain. The grief response most often does not feel like anything we would voluntarily invite into our life, and it certainly may not feel like a gift. So, why do we call grief a gift? Grief is a gift because it offers us healing and growth. Grieving provides the mechanism for processing painful emotions and healing wounded feelings while gaining insight that moves us from pain to peace, from hopeless to hopeful.

Our ability to heal and grow comes from moving through grief, which means moving through the feelings and emotions of loss. The GRACE model includes two helpful exercises to move you forward: 1. The GRACE Grief Model's "Grief Wave," and 2. The GRACE Grief Model's "3 Steps for Processing Feelings." The GRACE Grief Wave exercise in this unit can help you become aware of how you react to feelings and emotions associated with loss. The GRACE Grief Model's 3 Steps for Processing Feelings technique can then provide guidance on how to deal in healthy ways with the often-overwhelming feelings and emotions.

The GRACE model promotes and supports a key feature of healthy grieving, which is emotional flexibility. The 3 Steps for Processing Feelings is a useful tool for learning and practicing this flexibility, helping us become aware of and adapt to our emotional situations, including those realities that are difficult to tolerate. Emotional flexibility is what helps us respond in adaptive ways to the many emotions of grief, and emotional flexibility is what can prevent excessive avoidance and rumination.[62]

Using the 3 Steps for Processing Feelings, you will learn to: 1) Feel your feelings (promote and support awareness), 2) Name your feelings (validate emotions), and 3) Learn and grow from your feelings (process and heal). These steps can promote healing from losses big and small. Grief offers a kind of learning in which our brains are trying to solve a problem,[63] and our brains are seeking to arrive at a solution for that which was lost and to heal from the resulting emotions the loss created. The GRACE Grief Model's 3 Steps for Processing Feelings facilitates this learning and moves us closer to the healing we seek.

---

[62] O'Connor, 2023

[63] O'Connor, 2023

Serena and the Gift of Grief

When Serena's partner of almost 20 years decided to leave her, there were no discussions, no couples' therapy, just a simple good-bye. Serena was devastated. In one afternoon, her life and future as she knew it was turned upside down. Serena fell into deep despair and could not seem to shake the darkness of the depression that engulfed her. It was then she entered counseling. In our therapy sessions, Serena worked to process the many emotions that accompanied her grief. Applying the GRACE Model's 3 Steps for Processing Feelings, Serena learned to allow herself time and space to actually feel her emotions in a safe way, to name her emotions without judging them, and to learn and grow from these feelings.

One afternoon in therapy as we were working on step three (learning and growing from feelings), Serena had a breakthrough. Serena initially was only able to recognize one feeling, sadness. In time, however, she was able to feel and name many other feelings involving the loss of the relationship. Chief among these other feelings was anger. It was not until Serena allowed herself permission to truly feel how mad she was and identify that feeling as anger that she then was able to sit was this very uncomfortable feeling, allowing it to teach her and help her heal. She had to consider why she was so angry and at whom she was so angry. She learned that not only was she mad at her partner for leaving, but she also realized that she was mad at herself. Serena then was ready to recognize her own faults in the relationship. With this came regret but also a deeper understanding and acceptance, and ultimately healing. Once Serena was willing to allow herself to feel, name, and learn from her emotions, she was able to recover and move forward with her life feeling better equipped to enter a new relationship someday, more confident and healthier.

GRACE Grief Model: Grief Wave

Let us review the Grief Wave. As we discussed earlier, the Grief Wave illustrates how the feelings and emotions of loss move in and through our lives. Grief emotions are similar to waves rolling in and out of our lives, and at times these waves can roll over us, tumbling us to the ground. This wave metaphor is also helpful as we learn and practice the GRACE Grief Model 3 Steps for Processing Feelings, a process for helping us learn how to deal with the emotions of loss.

To begin, imagine you are on a seashore. It's a nice calm day.

Now imagine that you begin to feel grief, like a wave of emotion coming towards you.

Too often, rather than experiencing that wave of grief, we BLOCK that emotion or feeling.

But soon after, a new wave will come—another wave of grief arrives. And again, too often, we will continue blocking these new waves of feelings and emotions. We block our emotions and feelings in many ways, such as self-medicating, over-eating, over-working, etc.

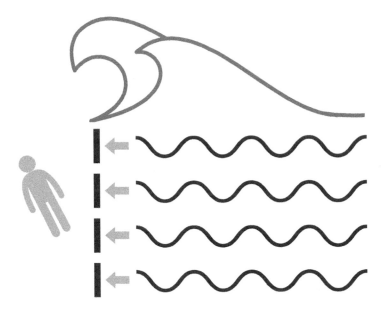

But the pattern continues . . . until finally the waves of feelings and emotions are simply too much, and they become like a tidal wave that can knock us down.

GRACE GRIEF MODEL:
3 STEPS FOR PROCESSING FEELINGS

The 3 Steps for Processing Feelings are a stepwise path for moving through grief emotions in a healthy way. These steps will support moving you from woundedness into a place of healing. Follow these steps in sequential order.

STEP 1: FEEL

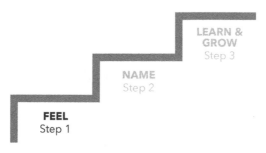

Support Awareness of Feelings and Healthy Expression of Feelings

Allow yourself some dedicated time to feel any feelings you may have associated with loss. (If you begin to feel too overwhelmed, stop and resume this exercise with your mental healthcare professional.) This is the time to express feelings, and to do so in healthy ways. Do not judge your feelings, just allow yourself to honestly feel whatever comes. For example, if you are truly sad and feel like crying, allow yourself to feel fully sad and cry.

STEP 2: NAME

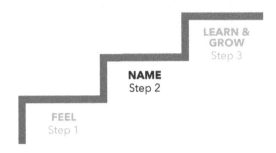

Validate Feelings

Write down each specific feeling you experienced from Step 1. Do not judge your feelings; just list them.

STEP 3: LEARN & GROW

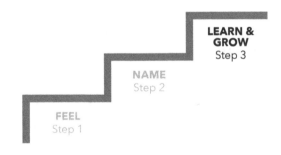

Process and Heal

Now that you have allowed yourself to feel your feelings and name each of those feelings, consider how these feelings and the information we associate with them may help us learn, grow, and heal. Remember, you are created of flesh and bones, but you are also created of stardust. You have atoms inside of your body that are billions of years old. There is a lot of innate wisdom in you! I believe our bodies are hard-wired to heal whenever possible, including from losses of all types. Just as a skinned knee will scab over or a broken bone will attempt to knit itself, our bodies were also created through time to heal from loss, and this is done through the process of adaptive grief work.

To facilitate learning and growth, ask yourself these questions:

- What insight can I glean from the feeling or feelings and by sitting with the accompanying emotions?

- Why might these specific feelings be coming to me now?

- Where are these feelings coming from and what caused the feelings?

- What wisdom might I gain from allowing myself time and space to actually feel and process each emotion associated with the loss?

- What might the feelings be teaching me?

- How can I learn and grow from the feeling and move towards healing?

PLANNING FOR GRIEF TRIGGERS

Triggers (often referred to as stressors) are actions or situations that can cause or contribute to adverse emotional reactions, which can result in initiating or worsening mental health issues.[64] A primary way to manage triggers is to accept the reality that grief triggers will occur and work to recognize these triggers in advance when possible. Know, however, not all triggers may be recognized in advance. When we are triggered and, perhaps especially for triggers that seem to take us by surprise, it is very helpful to have a plan for managing these triggers.

Having a plan of what to do before a trigger occurs can help ensure grief does not completely overwhelm and dysregulate you. The following

---

[64] Ponte, 2022

are examples of other peoples' plans to work through common grief triggers. Remember, these are only examples, and you will need to create your own workable plan that best fits with your healing.

Photos. After her son's death, it was too difficult for Anna to constantly see all the photos of her son that remained throughout every room of her house. Anna found it helpful to relocate many of these photos into her son's room until she was ready to again put the photos back out.

Songs. Sheila did not initially realize why she felt so melancholy on car rides until she recognized it was the songs on the car radio. Certain radio channels played music that reminded her (often subconsciously) of her ex-boyfriend. Sheila recognized this was happening and decided not to completely eliminate all the old triggering songs, but instead to add a few new music channels during her car ride to provide balance. Awareness and balance helped Sheila.

TV shows, movies, videos. Rafael was abused growing up and was often easily re-traumatized when watching graphic violent content. Rafael found it helpful to stop watching this content alone and instead worked with a therapist to process his trauma, which included helping him work through difficult graphic content.

Smells. Following the death of her mother, Rosalind was having a difficult time returning to worship in the church she grew up in. After a while, Rosalind was able to realize it was the fragrances within the church that were triggering her, specifically the incense often burned in the sanctuary area, which reminded her of her mother's funeral. Rosalind worked to understand this tie, address her unresolved grief about her mother, and was then able to successfully manage this trigger reaction.

Anniversary events. The first anniversary after Steve's retirement was much more difficult for him than he could have imagined. He was confused as to how he could be sad about the retirement he had worked towards for so long to achieve. Steve, however, was grieving the loss of not only his job, but also his work friends and his sense of meaning and purpose. Recognizing this and taking steps to find new ways to connect and find meaning were important for Steve.

Holidays. Thanksgiving used to be a wonderful time when Connie's large extended family gathered. However, Covid restrictions prevented the family from meeting on Thanksgiving for a couple years, and then soon after this family event simply started to fall apart as relatives no longer seemed able to make the time to travel. Each passing year, Connie longed for family Thanksgivings and began to deeply miss that time with her loved ones. Connie grew to dread the month of November and the approach of Thanksgiving. Connie then decided to begin new traditions that included seeing family during the other weeks of November and celebrating Thanksgiving day with her friends ("Friendsgiving").

Specific places. The hospital downtown was where Amilee delivered her baby, and where she would last hold her newborn child. Amilee had made the difficult decision upon news of her pregnancy that she would not keep the baby. Amilee wanted her baby to be raised by a family in a position to care and love her child in ways she currently was not. After the adoption, every time Amilee passed by the hospital area, she felt much sadness and regret. Amilee recognized the hospital was triggering her and, in time, she was able to work through her feelings about the adoption and eventually her pain was replaced by new feelings: hope and peace.

What are your grief triggers? Having awareness of your triggers and naming those triggers are important first steps towards drafting a personalized plan to calm the stressors that emotionally and physically provoke you in unhealthy ways. Using the examples provided above as a guide, name the triggers that are attached to your losses. Next, recognize how these triggers are impacting your thoughts, feelings, and behaviors (actions). Also, consider how your triggers impact your body. For example, when triggered do you experience headaches, muscle tightness, tremors, stomachaches, or other physical sensations?

When you are activated by a trigger, what helps calm the associated distressing thoughts, feelings, behaviors, and other concerning reactions? Now, add to your plan a list of healthy coping tools (e.g., breathwork, progressive muscle relaxation, taking a walk, listening to music, calling a friend, etc.) that you find helpful during triggering events and situations. Over time, you will want to continue expanding upon your plan as you gain greater awareness and insight into your personal triggers, as well as learn and adopt new healthy coping tools and skills.

Chapter 4

STEP 2: RE-STORY YOUR LOSS NARRATIVE

"Spiritual growth involves giving up the stories of your past so the universe can write a new one."

—MARIANNE WILLIAMSON

WIRED FOR STORIES

Humans are storytellers by design. Stories are how we learn to experience our world, make sense of our world, and share our world. Loss events are no exception. When we experience a loss, our brain attempts to create a story around the loss, including what happened, why it happened, how it happened, and how the loss impacts us. Storytelling is central to personal meaning-making and sense-making, as well as communal learning and shared experiences. It is through story that our brain creates and challenges assumptions, leading to the construction of beliefs.

Biochemically, storytelling releases chemicals, including cortisol, dopamine, and oxytocin, which support emotional regulation, keep us engaged in the narrative, and promote empathy.[65] Challenges, however, exist within the story creation process. Stories are equivalent to patterns, which our brain craves. It is in our brain's nature to tell stories and, when

---

[65] Peterson, 2017

we tell a completed story, our brain receives a dopamine reward. However, when we experience an incomplete story (faulty pattern recognition), the opposite can occur, a decrease in dopamine release.[66]

Yet not every story our mind constructs is true. One problem is that our mind will attempt to fill in blanks of a story as it seeks to complete a pattern. In this effort, however, our minds really can play tricks on us. Take the example of loss in which there is often a great amount of stimuli occurring around the loss event at different times—before, during, and after. At times, there is simply too much surrounding the loss for our brains to take in, and so our brains are left with puzzle pieces rather than a complete picture. Here, the brain will attempt to fill in the gaps with assumptions and even created memories. The result, a manufactured storyline that may miss important truths. Another challenge when constructing a story, one may fixate on certain details, as in cases of loss. It is as if our brain selects and hyper-focuses on narrow aspects of the loss story, which then forms a narrow problem-saturated version of the narrative we tell ourselves.

THE BRAIN AND STORYTELLING

Storytelling also affects us physiologically. When a loved one leaves, as in cases of death, divorce, separation, etc., this impacts our physical brain. To begin, when a bond is formed with someone we love, changes occur to the way proteins attach in the nucleus accumbens, impacting our brain's reward network so that neurons fire when our loved one approaches. The greater the bond, the more neurons are added, thus intensifying the reward network reaction in our brain. When we have love for someone, our brain encodes a bond that creates an overlapping "we" experience, not just a "you" and "me" experience.[67] Therefore, when a loved one is missing, we experience this as a part of us missing, much like an amputee experiences phantom pains.

---

[66] Burton, 2019

[67] O'Connor, 2022

MAPPING AND RE-MAPPING THE GRIEVED BRAIN

As we discussed in our introductory chapter, grief is a physiological and psychological process in the body. Many scientists view grief as a motivational process. Grief as a motivational state means that grieving involves yearning or reaching for something, moving towards something. Present fMRI imaging demonstrates the brain areas consistent with motivation and craving are the same primary brain areas activated in grief. This yearning, which is an earmark of the grief experience, remains engrained in our brain until our brain re-maps our relationship to the person or thing we have lost.

Consider research, including the work of O'Connor, Wellisch, Stanton, Eisenberger, Irwin, and Lieberman,[68] highlighting our brain's processing of pain and reward in which brain activity of persons experiencing grief demonstrates increased activity in the brain's pain center. Grief pain is not only mental, but also physical. Additionally, as with those with prolonged or complicated grief, the reward center of our brain (nucleus accumbens) is activated creating dopamine. Know that dopamine does not necessarily equate to making us feel good. Dopamine is associated with pushing us into a motivated state, creating within us desire. This desire can be healthy (I am hungry, so I need to eat) and unhealthy (an addict's desire for substance). The state of wanting activates the reward centers, which then moves us into two states: waiting and seeking. Our brain waits for the loss to resolve and seeks ways to hasten this process. When we experience a loss, our brain is mapped to include the now-lost person or thing.[69] This mapping includes space, time, and closeness—the three dimensions of a relationship.[70]

---

[68] O'Connor, Wellisch, Stanton, Eisenberger, Irwin, and Lieberman, 2008

[69] Huberman, 2022

[70] Huberman, 2022

After loss, how can we begin to re-map the brain to move through our grief and promote healing? The re-storying of our loss narrative is one powerful way to bring about the reframing or remapping of the relationship with who or what was lost. To support healthy remapping of the brain, re-storying will include continued attachment in healthy ways to the lost loved one or things. The memories, the feelings, the thoughts we have for the lost will continue. This library of memory and information we have created and captured over time about a loved one lost can support our re-mapping.[71] We can recall and remember the lost loved one, but we must uncouple the "old" library from current present bits of new information, feelings, and thoughts added to our brain's library.

For example, Mia's sister died in a plane crash on her way to visit Mia. Mia remains fixated on the notion "if only my sister wasn't coming to see me, she would never have died." This thought process is counter-factual and keeps Mia stuck in her grief process. Until Mia is able to uncouple this unhelpful thought from her loss story, she will remain stuck and not progress in her grief journey. A healthier re-frame for Mia might be to say, "My sister died in a plane crash that coincidentally happened to occur when she was on her way to visit me."

BIOCHEMISTRY OF GRIEF

Our loss narrative, therefore, is crafted by our brain's biochemistry, our mind's reactions and overreactions. The GRACE Grief Model blends elements of narrative therapy to examine the loss narrative to re-tell our story in ways that replace problem-saturated narratives with healthier integrated narratives allowing for the brain to incorporate feelings, emotions, and facts. This re-storying or re-telling supports a preferred narrative that offers unique outcomes and produces supportive healing for the grieving process.

---

[71] Huberman, 2022

For many, initial loss narratives were formed from feelings and emotions, but lack logic and reason. Many believe this occurs in cases where the amygdala (the brain's "emotional center") hijacks neuropathways and impedes connectivity to our prefrontal cortex (the brain's "logic center"). Others suggest the amygdala may not "hijack" these paths, but rather the amygdala continues to coordinate with (not dominate) the prefrontal cortex, and the emotional overreactions are the likely result of how we interpret or misinterpret situations.[72] Either way, the resulting effect on our narratives is the same: our loss stories become saturated with inaccuracies and misperceptions, which we continue to tell ourselves, and with each re-telling, we believe this problem-saturated loss version a little bit more. The goal in these cases is not to dismiss emotions, but rather to integrate emotion and feelings with logic, reason, and sound decision-making. In short, we need to calm down the overactive amygdala and incorporate logical, healthy thought using our prefrontal cortex, enabling us the opportunity to re-story our loss narrative with balance.

"THE PROBLEM"

In addition to supporting a healthier fuller narrative, narrative therapy also is helpful in that it conceptualizes people as separate from "the problem." In narrative therapy, problems are viewed as narrow and limiting client stories that do not align with the preferred experiences of self.[73] When I work with people whose loved one died, some therapeutic models (including CBT) would suggest we identify "the problem" within the person grieving (often this entails a diagnosis). However, "the problem" often lies not necessarily within the griever, as in the cases of a loved one dying. "The problem" is that their loved one died. Narrative therapy allows us to recognize and address the problem as separate from the person and does not pathologize grief.

---

[72] Dixon, 2023

[73] White & Epston, 1990; Williams-Reade, Freitas, & Lawson, 2014

GOALS OF RE-STORY

Goals of the "re-story" process (Step 2 in the GRACE Grief Model) are akin to those of narrative therapy, which include: support the re-authoring of stories through core processes that include deconstruction of problem-saturated stories, externalization of the story separating the client from the problem, mapping the effects of the problems, and re-authoring and creating a preferred narrative that offers unique outcomes and produces supportive networks for the client.[74] However, the GRACE Grief Model expands on narrative therapy goals in that the GRACE model also attempts to support re-mapping of the grieved brain to support adaptive healthy grieving.

Amare's Story

After Amare's wife died suddenly in a car accident, he developed clinical depression. Amare blamed himself for not driving her to the store that evening as she had requested. After her death, Amare feel into great despair and eventually Amare's sense of self began to suffer as he started to view himself as "the problem" in his grief story. Amare falsely grew to perceive he was the root-cause of not only his wife's death, but he believed he caused his own suffering and depression. Amare began thinking he would never be happy again and found himself isolating from friends and family as he started drinking to numb his pain. Amare needed help, including help realizing that he was not "the problem" in his grief story. In Amare's case, his faulty thinking (cognitive distortion) that he caused his wife's death needed to be addressed, as the actual root-cause of his depression was his wife's death (something he did not cause or have control over).

---

[74] White & Epston, 1990; Williams-Reade, Freitas, & Lawson, 2014

WRITING AND RE-WRITING
OUR GRIEF STORIES

As we move through our grief journey, we develop stories that we tell ourselves and others about our loss. Sometimes these stories are healthy and move us forward in our grief process, but sometimes they are unhealthy and keep us stuck in our grief. For many, it is time to examine or re-examine the stories we tell and, when needed, re-write our loss stories in fuller and healthier ways. Re-telling our stories in healthy ways does not mean forgetting about what happened or trying to change facts, rather it means adding important details and insights that bring deeper awareness and healing understanding. The practice of re-authoring stories and developing a preferred adaptive narrative is a goal of the GRACE Grief Model. Re-authoring includes "thickening" to create the new story.[75] One way re-authoring is achieved is through writings, including diary work, journaling, and letter writing.[76]

A STREET TO AVOID: LEARNING TO
RE-EXAMINE MY LOSS NARRATIVE

Every time I passed the street where my mother died, I would immediately feel sick to my stomach and I soon found myself avoiding that street and, eventually, that area altogether. It was not until I allowed myself to examine my loss narrative more fully that I was able to re-write my story with appropriate details and objective honesty, which allowed me to recall the whole story of the loss event concerning my mother's death. This examination enabled me to gain new valuable insight and perspective, including allowing me to once again view the positive aspects of her street, even amidst truthful pains and memories of death.

---

[75] White & Epston, 2009

[76] Thompson & Neimeyer, 2014

It was 2am when I received the call. My mother had coded. When I arrived, CPR was still being administered. Flashing lights and sirens assaulted my senses juxtaposed against a backdrop of quiet sleepy homes and calm purple skies. For months after my mother's death, I avoided going on or near the street where she died, thinking of this street and area only through the dark lens of death. I had been focused solely on the death event and this myopic view blinded me to a fuller truth. Through the process of re-telling my story, I was able to open to the whole truth— recalling the street before, during, and after my mother's death, all of the good and bad memories combined.

Through re-storying, I finally was able to again view the street and this area as beautiful and a fine place to visit, not a place to avoid. The actual street was, in fact, lovely. It was a tree-lined lane dotted with modest homes and small businesses brimming with life and people going about their day. I was able finally able to realize what a blessing it must have been for my mother to live on such a lovely street and even to have died on such a lovely street. While I did not forget the tragedy of my mother's death, my enriched loss narrative allowed me to open up to the fullness of the real story, including the beauty of the street and the wonderful and caring people on it who cared for my mother. So many truths I had obscured until I allowed myself to stop avoiding and stop focusing on just one aspect of the story, inviting a re-telling that opened me up to the whole truthful story. As my perspective about this street shifted, my unhealthy avoidance of the area faded, and my grieving processed forward in a healthier way.

"We can endure much more than we think we can; all human experience testifies to that. All we need to do is learn not to be afraid of pain. Grit your teeth and let it hurt. Don't deny it, don't be overwhelmed by it. It will not last forever. One day, the pain will be gone, and you will still be there."

—Rabbi Harold Kushner

Chapter 5

STEP 3: ADOPT NEW HEALTHY WAYS OF GRIEVING

IN THIS CHAPTER, WE will consider healthy ways to grieve through an examination of both culture and spirituality. We will explore the possibility of incorporating into our own grief processes some of the valuable adaptive lessons and tools we find throughout various cultures and through a deepening of our personal understanding of the sacred. Adopting new healthy ways of grieving can provide us with much needed tools to borrow and use, propelling us forward in our grief journey.

CULTURAL DIFFERENCES

"I remember walking slowly, head down, as I joined the others. We walked behind the casket from the church to the cemetery as the jazz band played. Some cried and some danced."

—MOURNER AT A NEW ORLEANS'
JAZZ FUNERAL PROCESSION

How do you grieve? Have you ever given much thought to what your own unique personal grief model looks like right now? Much of our grieving process is culturally based. Culture impacts grief in subtle and not so subtle ways. Some cultural responses to loss can be limiting and impede the grieving process, such as Eurocentric America's pattern of avoiding or minimizing grief,[77] while other cultural practices can prove healing, including those explored in this chapter. It is these healing practices from cultures near and far that I encourage you to discover and, when warranted, adopt into the rhythms of your own grieving patterns. We have much to share and learn from others. Drawing from different cultures helps connect us to a global wellspring of supportive traditions available for our use and healing as we move through our loss journeys.

Grief is a "transcultural phenomenon."[78] The stories we share about our losses are often impacted by cultural norms. Furthermore, the emotions of grief also differ across cultures. Grief, therefore, can be contextualized within what is deemed "acceptable" or "not acceptable" based on cultural values, beliefs, and ethics. While cultural complexities exist, prolonged grief or complicated grief has been well-defined and confirmed throughout a multitude of cultural ranges.[79] For example, although grief varies among cultures, it can be identified with reliability in grief assessments, including the Texas Revised Inventory of Grief (TRIG) and the Inventory of Complicated Grief (ICG).[80]

CULTURAL VARIANCES ON LOSS

Grief's cultural component can play a large part in what is considered a loss, as well as how one grieves.[81] Grief's spiritual component, which can vary widely according to culture, can enable people to create meaning-making from loss and employ spiritual coping skills in relationship

---

[77] Tyler & Darrow, 2022

[78] Enez, 2018, p. 277

[79] Enez, 2018

[80] Enez, 2018, Maercker & Znoj, 2010

[81] Prieto, 2011

to a person's faith beliefs and the outcome of their major life events.[82] As demonstrated in research on the Muscogee Creek tribe,[83] grief in Chinese families,[84] and bereavement in Mexican American families,[85] an individual and community's expression of grief can be heavily influenced by factors of culture flowing from variances in tradition and social norms.[86]

PROLONGED GRIEF AS CROSS-CULTURAL

Current research indicates prolonged grief is present across cultures, including those cultures with varied perspectives and rituals on death and loss. In cases of suspected prolonged grief, culture and religion are factors to be considered before reaching a diagnosis. Both culture and religion can be determining factors in assessing normal grief from prolonged grief.[87] Of note, some researchers assert it is impossible to discern normal grief from prolonged grief because of their general similarities combined with discriminating for cultural variances.[88]

DIVERSE CULTURES & DIVERSE WAYS OF GRIEVING

Grief traditions can vary greatly across cultural traditions. We see evidence of this throughout grief work in every country. Some examples of grief traditions across cultures (including spiritual cultures) include New Zealand's Māori tribal Haka dance often performed at funerals; Mexico's *Dia De Los Muertos* celebratory holiday of remembrance for

---

82 Matthews & Marwit, 2006

83 Walker, 2008

84 Ho & Brotherson, 2007

85 Doran & Hanson, 2006

86 Montano et al., 2016.

87 Shear et al., 2011

88 Miyabayashi & Yasuda, 2007

those deceased; the Hindu's sharing of a special meal to memorialize a loved one's passing and affirm their belief in reincarnation; Vietnamese's shrines adorned with photos, special items, and candles created in memory of deceased loved ones; and the New Orleans' jazz funeral marches that form a parade, led by the casket, taking mourners from the church to the cemetery.

Grief traditions are not the only variation, there also seem to exist cultural variations in how people express grief emotion, which has been recognized for a long time. Decades ago, Barley, writing on the subject of culture and grief, stated that in cases of bereavement Westerners mourn "not a ritual, social or physical state but one of disordered emotions that may require therapy," while "the dominant emotion at a Chinese funeral may not be grief but scarcely concealed fear of the contagion of death." This emotion may perhaps resonate more now with Westernized mourners in light of the COVID-19 pandemic of 2020.

Religious beliefs influenced by culture also impact grief traditions. "Religious beliefs and practices…are strongly related to culture and may account for some of the variations in grieving processes." For example, as we again examine Chinese tradition, we find influence of fatalism affecting Chinese bereavement as marked by a culture of infrequent sharing of grief emotions. In fact, for the traditional Chinese, the sharing of grief emotion is atypical. The way many Chinese comfort mourners is by saying, "Restrain your grief and accord with inevitable changes."[89]

INDIVIDUAL & COMMUNAL GRIEF ASPECTS: GENDER, CULTURE, BIOLOGY & ENVIRONMENT

When discussing emotions, it is important to acknowledge individual and communal aspects. Individually and communally, emotional

---

[89]   Stelzer et al., 2020, p. 4

variance among people may be explained in part due to gender (biological sex at birth), culture, biology, and environment. Gender differences in emotions are observed and, as some studies suggest, women show stronger emotional expressiveness whereas men have stronger emotional experiences relative to specific types of emotions, namely anger and positive stimuli. Women are reported to experience more intense emotional responses overall, especially pertaining to negative emotions, whereas men are reported to experience stronger emotional experiences.[90] More on this will be explored in the upcoming chapter.

According to Nangyeon Lim,[91] emotion, whether viewed as universal or social, is in large part biologically based and also influenced by environment. Some research suggests that the biological basis of emotion involves genetic similarities across culture, such as facial expressions (e.g., smile when happy, frown when mad, etc.) which can be interpreted similarly regardless of culture or geographical location.[92] Culture's impact on emotion is broad and can shape the words and expressions used to describe emotions,[93] as well as how emotions are expressed.[94]

[90] Deng et al., 2016

[91] Lim, 2016

[92] Lim, 2016; Eckman, 1972

[93] Lim, 2016; Shott, 1979

[94] Lim, 2016; Heelas, 1986

Miguel y Familismo

Miguel's bills mounted up, especially after a prolonged absence from work due to a diagnosis of Long Covid. Struggling with financial woes, dealing with Covid's lasting effects which included brain fog, constant fatigue, and lung impairment, things seemed like they couldn't get worse, but they did. Miguel's company announced his position would be eliminated, leaving him with no means of financial support and no health benefits. With rent due, a bank account nearly depleted, and a near-empty refrigerator, most people facing Miguel's circumstances might have felt overwhelmed, yet Miguel did not. Why?

Miguel was raised within a Latino collectivist culture that places strong value on family—familismo. It is part of his family's culture to care and protect one another, especially during hard times. Miguel found great comfort knowing his family would help provide for him. The scope of familismo goes beyond immediate family to include extended family members (aunts/tias, uncles/tios, cousins/primos y primas, etc.) who collectively offer necessary help to provide for those within la familia (the family). Thanks to his cultural framework, even though Miguel struggled with the loss of his health, his job, and financial independence, he still felt supported and cared for, which in turn promoted his healing and resiliency.

MEANING-MAKING:
A FRAMEWORK FOR SPIRITUALITY

Recalling the work of neuroscience from earlier chapters, we understand our brain maps attempt to link us to lost loved ones within the three dimensions of a relationship: space, time, and closeness.[95] In cases of death, our brain still desires to locate the loved one in a specific place and time, begging the question "Where are they?" Spirituality can help create a new understanding of where our deceased loved one now exists in space and time, and this can facilitate the re-mapping of the brain in healthy ways that support the grieving process. For example, spirituality may better enable a person to re-orient their relationship to a deceased person, which may place the deceased as now existing in eternity (time) and in the realm understood as heaven (place). Or spirituality, for others, may allow an understanding that the deceased exists for now (time) scattered in the universe as stardust (place).

It remains constant that a primary goal of grieving is to heal. The goal of healing aims to make one more whole, thus more *holy*.[96] Often when healing, we must remain in part of the pain. Part of the counselor's work includes helping the client both remain in and travel through pain, which can be supported through practices such as prayer, meditation, mindfulness, and rituals. "Living a spiritual life necessarily involves transforming suffering into compassion both for oneself and for others."[97] Blending grief into a framework of spirdualty opens up the possibility for one's loss journey to benefit from one's search for the sacred.

---

[95] Huberman, 2022

[96] Cashwell & Young, 2011

[97] Cashwell & Young, 2011; Vardey, 1995

Spirituality is any way of relating to that which is sacred or to a greater reality.[98] Religion is a subset of the spiritual and involves culturally bound or institutional ways of relating to the sacred. Many argue that the terms spiritual and religious should be separated. However, for the purpose of this document, spiritual will remain the umbrella terminology within which matters of religion, faith, and beliefs will be discussed.

Spirituality can effect one's understanding of grief as well as provide coping resources in dealing with loss. Participation in spiritual practices (e.g., worship, memorial services, sitting shiva, etc.) can provide an understanding of loss that includes meaning-making around loss and extends support through the grieving process to those impacted by the loss. Other spiritual disciplines and practices, such as meditation and prayer (which can be individual or communal), also have been proven to provide help for those in grief by providing comfort.[99]

The GRACE Grief Model incorporates spirituality in the form of meaning-making, specifically the GRACE model adopts aspects of Crystal Park's Meaning-making Model. Park's Meaning-making Model offers a theoretical plan that attempts to make sense of existing meaning-making theory and research while targeting meaning, spirituality, and stress-related growth.[100]

Park's model focuses on the influence of global meaning (what people believe and want) as related to people experiencing stressful or traumatic situations (e.g., grief and complicated grief). Park views spirituality as a "common source of global meaning," and defines spirituality with a seemingly close kinship to religiousness. Park affirms a view of religion as "a search for significance in ways related to the sacred,"[101] and asserts

---

[98] Rosmarin, 2018

[99] Block, 2017

[100] Park, 2013

[101] Park, 2011, p. 409; Pargament, 1997

that this definition of religiousness underscores meaning. For Park, spirituality offers helpful illustrations of the myriad of ways global meaning is conjectured. According to Park, "spirituality can inform all aspects of global meaning,"[102] including the shaping of beliefs and offering incentive and goal setting for life in ways that support a person's sense of purpose.

Spirituality is specifically and intentionally incorporated into Park's meaning-making model (MMM). The MMM "demonstrates how spirituality, a core aspect of global meaning for many, is related to health and involved in dealing with serious illness (e.g., prolonged grief)."[103] Park views spirituality and religion as "protective factors" in one's health and wellbeing,[104] and asserts spirituality can impact ones understanding of grief.[105] A long-standing problem is that, despite most Americans claiming belief in God, the majority of psychotherapists and other mental health-care professionals "lack even rudimentary training in how to address spirituality and religion in treatment."[106] In offering a spiritual-minded grief model, psychotherapists and their clients will benefit.

Research has affirmed links between spirituality and positive bereavement adjustments. Park asserts that global meaning is comprised of beliefs, goals, and a sense of meaningfulness or purpose. Beliefs, according to Park, encompass core schemas involving matters such as justice, control, predictability, and coherence. For those for whom spirituality is significant, spirituality is therefore inherently part of their beliefs and goals.[107]

---

[102] Park, 2013, pg. 42

[103] Park, 2013, pg. 45

[104] Park, 2007, p. 313

[105] Wortmann & Park, 2008

[106] Rosmarin, 2018, p. 2

[107] Wortmann & Park, 2009

SPIRITUALITY IN PSYCHOTHERAPY

A growing body of evidence has suggested incorporating social aspects of religion and spiritually with attention to the individual's identity and relationship paradigms is helpful for a fuller investigation of the self within the psychotherapeutic relationship.[108] Research points to religion and faith as helping grievers, including those bereaved, by providing meaning and coping.[109] Those experiencing loss often turn to meaning-making within a spiritual context. In the case of bereavement, 80 percent of Americans believe in some form of afterlife.[110]

SPIRITUALITY IN AMERICA

The topic of spirituality directly relates to most people in this country. Per a Gallup Poll conducted in 2022, 81 percent of Americans stated belief in God. Another study conducted in 2017 stated that 80 percent of Americans affirm belief in God, with 55 percent meaning a faith in God and 23 percent espousing a faith in a higher being.[111]

Benefits and Limitations

Religion has both identified benefits and limitations regarding grief work. Religion has been proven to correlate with more positive attitudes and better life satisfaction for many.[112] However, literature also suggests religiosity for some can have harmful effects and exacerbate mental health issues, like guilt, obsessions, and rigid thought.[113]

---

[108] Tummala-Narra, 2009

[109] Matthews & Marwit, 2006

[110] Pew Forum, 2018

[111] Pew Forum, 2018

[112] Dura-Vila, Littlewood, & Levey, 2013

[113] Dura-Vila, Littlewood, & Levey, 2013

SPIRITUALITY: A MISSING ASPECT IN MOST GRIEF MODELS

While there exists a recognized need to incorporate spirituality, research has demonstrated that most grief models fail to include the spiritual. There are models, such as William Worden's *Tasks of Mourning*, which acknowledge the value of spiritual incorporation. For example, Worden mentions spiritual integration in his third task of identifying meaning of loss and adjusting spiritually to that loss. Worden himself expressed his concern that therapists and researchers are failing to appreciate "the uniqueness of the grief experience," adding that a one-size model of grief treatment is "restrictive."[114]

Yet Worden's task model seems to lack instruction on how to adopt individual spirituality as part of the grief journey. Of note, the GRACE Grief Model Workbook, a companion piece to this book, provides insight and exercises on how to include one's individual spirituality into the grief healing journey.

SPIRITUALITY AND GRIEF RESEARCH

Spirituality matters, including matters of faith, religion, and belief encompass numerous dimensions. These varied dimensions impact understandings of loss and loss-related research. To more fully understand and investigate how grief is impacted by spiritualty's complexities, researchers must attend to important aspects such as a relationship with God and views of the Divine, spiritual emotions and attachments, and more.[115] A person who is grieving may be impacted, for example, by their denomination as their faith tradition informs their understanding of the

---

[114] Worden, 2018

[115] Park & Halifax, 2011

loss and how they grieve that loss. Research has affirmed links between spirituality and positive bereavement adjustments.[116]

SPIRITUALITY AND MEANING-MAKING

Again, spirituality can impact ones understanding of grief as well as provide coping resources in dealing with loss.[117] Park asserts that global meaning is comprised of beliefs, goals, and sense of meaningfulness or purpose. Beliefs, according to Park, encompass core schemas involving matters such as justice, control, predictability, and coherence. As previously stated, for those for whom spirituality is significant, spirituality is inherently part of their beliefs and goals.[118]

Juana's Story

Juana once held the belief that her husband's death by drowning in flood waters was a punishment from God. However, following her husband's funeral, she began visiting with the faith leader at her place of worship and, in time, Juana grew to understand her husband died not because of any type of punishment by God, but rather because there are natural laws that exist in our universe and these natural laws have natural consequences. Juana was able to consider alternate perspectives as to why her husband died, and her belief shifted from a "punishment by God" theory to believing her husband's death resulted from him begin caught in flood waters caused by unexpected torrential rains. Her shift allowed her to move forward in her grieving process and also to reconnect to God in ways that were meaningful for her.

---

[116] Wortmann & Park, 2008

[117] Park, 2013; Wortmann & Park, 2008

[118] Wortmann & Park, 2009

SPIRITUALITY AND FUNERALS

How are funerals or memorial services handled in your spiritual or faith-based tradition? In the Christian tradition, when someone dies, church members and clergy reach out and offer comfort to the surviving family members. During this time, funeral arrangements are often discussed. A funeral or memorial service is typically held at a church or funeral home. Oftentimes, there is a wake or visitation held the night prior to the funeral service. Following the funeral, attendees proceed to the place of burial or interment for a short grave-side service. Afterwards, a reception offering food and beverages to attendees is often provided at either the church or the home of the bereaved family members.

For many Christians, these events occur during roughly a one-week period. For Protestants, this often marks the end of the formal tradition supporting bereavement. However, in other faith traditions (Christian and non-Christian), these rituals can be much longer and more involved. One example is the Eastern Orthodox Church's practice of mourning, which extends for 40 days in general and lasts for one year for close relatives. In this Orthodox custom, there are also memorials for the deceased celebrated at three months, six months, nine months, one year, and on the anniversary date of the death for a minimum of seven years.

Jewish tradition provides another example of extended bereavement rituals. In Jewish culture, death is viewed as a normal part of the continuum of the life cycle, and a present part of every life. Death is incorporated into culture by its mention in daily Jewish prayer and services, and through marking times of remembrance throughout the Jewish calendar year. The Jewish life cycle extends into death, including pre-burial (Aninut), the first week after death (Shiva), the first month after a death (Shloshim), the first year after a death (Shanah), and extends to include loss across one's entire life. During shiva, community members continually offer support to the family of the deceased in the form of prayer, food, and sharing stories about the deceased.

In Buddhist traditions, there is no standardized death or funeral rites. Often, individual Buddhists will simply follow the funeral rituals of the country in which they live, which can include cremations, traditional burials, or water burials. The Buddhist funerals are often held in a monastery or a home, and Buddhist monks may be invited to officiate the ceremony. Mourners often place candles, flowers, or fruit near the body. Tibetan Buddhists may follow the Tibetan Sky Burial in which the deceased's body is allowed to be consumed by nature on a mountaintop and loved ones read to the deceased from the Bardo Thodol (the Tibetan Book of the Dead) for the purpose of helping the deceased accept and transition into death. The Buddhist mourning periods vary, but traditionally last 49–100 days, with services held on day three, day 49 (the period believed to achieve rebirth), and day 100.

The Islam funeral service is a prayer service called the Salat Janazah. There are no wakes, visitations, or viewings because the body is buried as soon as possible. Islam tradition always buries the deceased (no cremations) and positions the body facing towards Mecca with the belief the body remains in the coffin until Judgment Day. Islamic funerals are community events. However, in some Islamic countries, women are discouraged from attending because of concerns their mourning may be too expressive. After the funeral, mourners spend the day together typically at a home and share a meal. The traditional mourning period is forty days, and some modern Muslim communities observe a shorter mourning period. During the Islamic mourning period, community members bring food and offer support.

In the Hindu tradition, funeral rites (*antyesti*) come from scriptures called the *Vedas*. This practice commonly includes cremation, whereby fire is seen as a type of purification from this life into the next life. Hindus believe the deceased will be either reincarnated or reach moksha (becoming one with Brahman, a divine force and supreme reality). A few days after cremation, the ashes of the body are scattered in a body of water, signifying a final separation between body and soul. Mourning periods in Hindu tradition vary from ten days to one month. The 13th day of mourning is marked by a ceremony to release the soul of the loved one, and on the first one-year anniversary of the deceased's passing, a feast or dinner is held in the deceased's honor.

"FORGET ME NOT"

This story, about my stepmother Judy, speaks to how we remain beautifully tethered together in this lifetime and beyond. This narrative reminds us that even after the death of a loved one, at least two things remain: the relationship and the love.

Judy had served as a public-school teacher for over three decades with a reputation for helping even the most challenging students to improve. She was firm, fair, and always reliable. It was December when Judy learned her cancer had returned, but this time it was terminal. She knew her time was short, but no one told her she would have less than three months to live. Her concerns were not for herself, but rather for her family and her students. Highly intelligent and gifted in many areas, she could have selected any career path. Judy chose to dedicate herself to teaching out of a deep sense of purpose and a belief that helping children improve is the best way to help our world improve.

Her final months included times of deep concern for her students Did I do enough for my students? Was I too firm? Was I too soft? Will my students even remember me 20 years from now? On a cold February day, Judy passed surrounded by loved ones. She had a sweet funeral ceremony in her hometown church. The sanctuary was packed. So many teachers and students wanted to attend Judy's funeral that the school had to close the day of her funeral. At the conclusion of the ceremony before the closing of the casket, one of Judy's students quietly approached her casket and slipped into it a photo of themselves with a simple thank-you. The student later shared with a family member the reason why they left their photo: "I didn't want her to forget me."

Judy's worldview included a sense of purpose around serving and educating children and youth, and a faith-filled belief that her efforts could make a positive difference in the world. While she spent most of her life helping and educating, I cannot help but wonder if Judy knew before her passing how much she impacted others.

It has been decades since her death and Judy's students are now grown, most with children of their own. Through the years, this beautiful truth remains—not only have Judy's students not forgotten her, but many keep her alive through living out the lessons she taught and by sharing stories about her. This yearning to both *remember* and *be remembered* by those we care about finds hope in a tethering that occurs between people, a tethering to one another in this life and beyond this life. Even in death, there remains a connection through the ties that bind us—these ties are the relationship and the love. Even after death, the relationship (albeit greatly changed) and the love not only continue, but can grow in healthy ways. From a biological perspective, the loved one who dies remains literally with us as part of us because our brain's wiring includes this bond.[119]

---

[119] O'Connor, 2022

Frances' Letter: A Prayer for Generations

Prayer, in its broadest terms, is a form of conversation, a way to relate to the sacred, to acknowledge a Higher Power, and prayer can also be a position of mindfulness and meditation. Prayer, in its many forms, has been utilized throughout human existence to speak to the Divine, the great unknown, a way to connect to the sacred across a great divide. Prayer, too, can be used to reach across generations.

Frances was a kind soul. Born in a small home in the Texas countryside, she was never one to ask for much, keeping but very few material possessions. Frances was my grandmother and one of my very favorite people who, at times, raised me. When her own children (my mother, aunt and uncle) were very young, she wrote a prayer to God. It was a mother's plea asking God to watch over her children and asking for the Divine to guide her as she cared for and raised them. The prayer was handwritten in ink on a small piece of scrap paper and was for many years kept tucked away. After Frances passed, my mother kept that prayer with her all her life. Later, when my mother passed, I then became the steward of this family prayer.

Frances' prayer was penned almost 80 years ago, but her heartfelt words still echo in my life today, just as relevant as the day she wrote them. I now keep the prayer in a frame in my office where I see it daily. Her prayer reminds me of the love parents have for their children and that words spoken to the Divine can move through time and space in ways we can only imagine. Her sweet prayer reminds me also of this beautiful truth: prayers don't expire.

SPIRITUALITY AND FORGIVENESS

For those who are grieving, forgiveness can often be part of the journey towards healing. In my work with people struggling with loss, I recognize many different feelings expressed. Frequently, those feelings include anger and guilt. Regina came to me holding much anger. She expressed feeling mad at her dead husband for dying and leaving her alone, and she was also angry at the cancer that took his life. After Serena's long-term relationship ended, she spoke of the guilt she carried for having an affair that caused the rupture. While Regina and Serna had different loss experiences and different feelings, both Regina and Serena needed to work on the same thing: forgiveness. (Of note, the topic of forgiveness is a complex subject that will not be fully unpacked in the scope of this work, but I do aim to bring forgiveness into this conversation.)

Lack of forgiveness stalls healing, lack of forgiveness derails peace. Forgiveness of others and forgiveness of self can take time and may be difficult, but forgiveness can offer life-giving healing and help move you forward on your grief journey. Forgiveness includes a choice, and the choice to forgive or not forgive shapes us and our life.[120] In cases where someone has been wronged, forgiveness of another (the offender) does not minimize, eliminate, or excuse the wrong done, rather, forgiveness is a choice the offended person makes to no longer be victimized by the wrong done to them. Forgiveness is a letting go, a decision to unshackle ourselves and keep unshackling ourselves from the torments caused by wrong doings. Sometimes the wrongs are things done to us and sometimes the wrongs are things we have done.

Forgiveness is a construct shared between the secular and religious/spiritual worlds. The concept of forgiveness is a key principle in all major religions, yet each religion offers their own understanding and

---

[120] Payne, 2024

practice. Forgiveness within a Jewish informed perspective seems to prioritize repentance of the offender, whereas a Christian informed perspective seems to extend forgiveness as a virtue without repentance. Islam speaks of forgiveness with a correlation to retaliation and punishment,[121] but, drawing from the Quran, Islam also states the highest virtue is to forgive and offer mercy, even toward the enemy.[122] From the Hindu tradition, forgiveness is truth. Quotes from the Hindu religious text the Mahabharata state, "Forgiveness is truth…this world is upheld by forgiveness."[123] Buddhism is viewed as a "religion of forgiveness."[124] According to Buddhist sacred writing, "Hatred does not cease by hatred at any time: hatred ceases by love. This is an unalterable law."[125, 126]

In the case of Regina and Serena, both held religious beliefs and we found ways to incorporate their individual spirituality into their work on forgiveness. For Regina, leaning into her Buddhist tradition and focusing on love of self and love of others allowed her to ultimately forgive. Similarly, Serena found much comfort in the teachings of Catholicism and was also eventually able to reach a place of forgiveness, beginning with self-forgiveness.

> "The LORD is close to the brokenhearted and saves those who are crushed in spirit."
>
> —PSALM 34:18

---

[121] Katergga & Shenk, 1981

[122] Ansari, 1970; Webb, Toussaint, & Conway-Williams, 2012

[123] Prakash, 1985, p. 227–228; Webb, Toussaint, & Conway-Williams, 2012

[124] Gour, 1929, p. 385

[125] Dhammapada 1:3–5

[126] Easwaran, 2007b; Webb, Toussaint, & Conway-Williams, 2012

✳ Chapter 6

STEP 4: CONNECT WITH SELF & OTHERS

"Connection is why we're here; it is what gives purpose and meaning to our lives."

—BRENE BROWN

W E ARE CREATED FOR connection. Within our individual biology, our atoms link and cells combine. Our bodies are organized to interconnect from within as systems. Externally, we find the very nature of humanity is connection. We seek others for support and survival, and to share our world with. Connecting with ourselves and others supports the grief journey. In this chapter, we will explore connection during times of loss, including connecting with ourselves, connecting with friends and family, and connecting with professional support. Connecting with oneself can include an examination of who we are in light of loss. For some, this cuts to the core of not just merely how we view ourselves considering the loss event, but how this loss shapes or re-shapes our very identity. Connecting to others, such as friends and family, helps us acknowledge our human need for community. Finally, connection at times will include reaching out to professionals for support, including during times of loss.

CONNECTING WITH SELF

Self and Identity

When Jennifer's fiancé died, she found herself in a state of identity ambiguity. She no longer felt like a single person, yet since her fiancé died before the wedding, she also did not feel like a married person. Jennifer struggled not just with the loss of her beloved fiancé, but also with who she now was as framed by the loss. Was Jennifer a "widow?" Was Jennifer a "fiancé?" Jennifer viewed herself as a "widowed-fiancé." Further, her once solid support system of friends seemed to be falling apart. Prior to her engagement, Jennifer's friend group had been shifting from single friends towards married friends. After the fiancé's death, Jennifer found both groups slowly retreating, as they seemed to find it now difficult to be around Jennifer. She, too, found it difficult. Being around her married friends was now painful and being around her single friends felt inauthentic to how she viewed herself. For Jennifer, staying stuck in the role of "widowed-fiancé" resulted in stagnation. Working through how she viewed herself was an important part of helping her not only grieve her fiancé, but also in helping her form and re-form connections post-loss. Connecting with who we are—our identity—in light of our loss event can help support our healing journey.

Self and Gender Considerations

Connecting with self also includes a realization of how gender identity may impact the grief process. For example, while increasingly many adults who identify as men in Westernized cultures feel more comfortable talking about loss and sharing grief emotions, there remains a pervasive reluctance among some in this population to share their grief experience. For adult males who evade or minimize their grief, this can result in potential delays in grief responses and delays in grief processing. Despite greater understanding and efforts to de-stigmatize male expressions of emotions, there remains much work to be done towards a broader acceptance of men demonstrating the fullness of their feelings, including grief emotions.

Traditional research suggests that men feel an expectation to hide their own emotions and remain emotionally strong for others, even despite trending changes in social attitudes regarding traditional male roles. When men do share their feelings about loss, they often do so in culturally normed "masculine" ways.[127] Cultural beliefs as to gender stereotypes (how men and women "should" be) still continue in part due to gendered cultural roles that promote certain subsequent behaviors, including how one expresses grief. In Western cultures, women tend to hold communal roles, which require relational and emotional expression, whereas men often have agentic roles, which promote independence and self-reliance. Also, it is theorized that men's decreased opportunities for social support may explain why males in general are more reluctant than women to share emotional experiences.[128] A more recent examination of how men actually speak about loss (the words they use and stories they constrict) suggests less of a gap. Studies of linguistic markers for grief demonstrate men and women are actually more similar than different in how they create their grief narrative.[129]

While both men, women, and nonbinary persons are impacted by loss and the resulting grief, research indicates those who identify as women are especially at risk for grief complications. Specifically, adult females are at higher risk for developing grief, and higher risks of developing severe psychological symptomology related to grief.[130] For example, bereaved

---

[127] McCreight, 2004

[128] Stelzer et al., 2019

[129] Stelzer et al., 2019

[130] Chiu et al., 2011

women are more likely to suffer from depression symptoms than men.[131] In general, women are found to be more significantly impacted by pathological processes of grief,[132] including severe anxiety and depression.[133] This increase in pathology leads to women's overall increased risk of developing complicated grief (a form of grief with potentially serious consequences). Research suggests, greater attention should be paid to grieving females as a high-risk group.[134]

Those who experience the loss of a same-gender partner report greater psychological distress than differently-gendered bereaved partners.[135] Some research indicates poorer bereavement outcomes for gay, lesbian, and bisexual persons.[136] Struggles in this community include disenfranchised grief in which their losses, as in the loss of a partner or spouse, are not taken as seriously by some groups as the losses of heterosexual persons. Further, socially excluded populations, including many in the LGBTQ+ community, often have poorer access to care. Yet not enough attention has been paid to this marginalized community even though they are at increased risk of certain life-limiting illnesses and may not receive the care and support they need at the end of life and into bereavement.[137]

SELF AND CULTURE

In Chapter 5, we explored how culture impacts the grief experience and we looked at some of the ways other cultures handle loss. Here, I again want to remind you of the importance that incorporating culture can be

---

[131]　Chen, Ying, Ingles, et al. 2020

[132]　Kersting & Kroker, 2009

[133]　Chiu et al., 2011; Neria et al., 2007

[134]　Chiu et al., 2011

[135]　Timmons, Pittman, King et al., 2023

[136]　Pitman, King, Gao, Johnson, Yu, & Harding, 2022

[137]　Bristow, Marshall, & Harding, 2016

in your grieving process. Your own individual experience and expression of grief can be heavily influenced by factors of culture flowing from variances in tradition and social norms.[138] For these reasons, it is necessary to examine your own culture balanced with your own personal understandings and traditions regarding loss and grief. Your cultural traditions and norms combined with how you choose to live into (or not live into) these can heavily influence how you grieve.

Samira's Story

Samira, who was born in India and moved to America as a young adult, was 54 years old when her father died. Samira's family, most of whom still lived in India, elected to have her father's remains cremated in keeping with their family's customs. During her time in the U.S., she attended funeral services of those from different cultures, including services in which the bodies were buried rather than cremated. Samira found comfort in the idea of going to a cemetery plot to mourn. In time, she grew to prefer the practice of burial and shared with her family her new preference that, someday after her own passing, she wanted to be buried instead of cremated. Her family did not understand and was upset with her choice.

For most of Samira's life, she readily adapted the beliefs and values of her homeland India, as well as her traditional Hindu teachings and customs. However, after living in the United States for many years, Samira found herself at times in conflict with some of her previously held cultural norms, including the custom favoring cremation. (Of note, not all Indians or Hindus

---

[138] Montano et al., 2016

practice cremation, but this was the tradition within Samira's family.) At times, Samira's changing personal values and beliefs were at odds with Indian and Hindu traditions, as well as with the cultural traditions of her own family.

Samira continued to work through her cultural understandings from both a personal and communal perspective. She eventually grew to appreciate that, according to her own beliefs, neither choice—burial or cremation—was necessarily "right" or "wrong." Samira realized her personal need after the death of a loved one was to visit their remains in a cemetery, yet she was also able to retain appreciation for her family's tradition of cremation. For Samira, a healthy way forward was to blend communal cultural norms with her own personal understandings, which included creating for her a new tradition, one that accepted and permitted burial.

CONNECTING WITH OTHERS

Connecting with Friends, Family, and Community

Humankind was created to live and be in community, and humankind was created to heal in community. At times, working through our grief alone can be good and even necessary, yet it is also important to incorporate into our healing process a community, including friends, family, and, when needed, professionals. Friends and family offer important and essential support during times of loss. Those we entrust into our circles during times of pain bear that loss alongside us by sitting with us, often holding our hand, listening, offering empathy, and encouraging us. Our community of supporters also helps coordinate other means of help, such as bringing meals, caring for our home (e.g., mowing our yard or helping with laundry), watching other family members (e.g., babysitting children or helping care for elderly or disabled family members), and helping pay for various expenses incurred during times of loss. Friends and family are frequently the first line of support that comes to our rescue.

There are also other types of communties which provide much needed support during loss, including groups with whom we associate. For example, school teachers collectively grieve losses within their teacher groups and professional associations, including after great losses experienced from tragic school schootings. Following the horrific school shooting on May 24, 2022 at Robb Elementary in Uvalde, Texas in which 19 students and two teachers were killed, teachers near and far gathered informally and formally to support the victims, the school families, fellow teachers, and many others who were impacted by this devastating and senseless act of violence.

Communal grieving is also part of many cultures. These norms vary across location. Westernized cultures may want to talk about the grief feelings amongst their groups, whereas, other cultures, such as South Koreans, tend to offer comfort to the bereaved through actions rather than words.[139] In Jewish tradition, the practice of sitting shiva litterally, emotionally, and spiritually joins mourners together, as community members come to sit at the home of the bereaved following the death.

Connecting with Mental Health Professionals

Everyone grieves and our grief can range from mild, to moderate, to severe. At any level of grief, if you feel you want or need additional support, reach out to a mental healthcare practitioner. These professionals are skilled at educating you and helping you through life's losses. Professionals trained in mental healthcare include your medical doctor,

---

[139] Franco & Yang, 2020

psychiatrist, psychologist, licensed professional counselor (LPC), licensed marriage and family therapist (LMFT), and social worker.

Connecting with Faith and Spiritual Leaders

Some may prefer to also talk about their loss with a trusted faith or religious leader, such as a minister, pastor, rabbi, imam, or spiritual guide. In addition to reaching out to your own personal faith or spiritual leader, another resource to consider is the National Alliance on Mental Illness (NAMI). NAMI offers a non-religious interfaith resource network called FaithNet. FaithNet (nami.org/Get-Involved/NAMI-FaithNet) serves to promote the role of spirituality in the lives of those living with a mental health condition.

Connecting with Support Groups

Specialized support groups that focus on grief, including groups for prolonged grief, can be very useful in the grief journey. Being with others who are also experiencing loss can promote your own healing and benefit others in the group at the same time. To grieve effectively, some research suggests that those battling bereavement should seek to join groups with others experiencing a similar loss.[140] For example, combat veterans will want to find a group comprised of other combat vets, whereas, women grieving from the loss of a child should locate groups of other women whose children have died.[141] Speak with your medical doctor or mental healthcare provider to see if a support group might be right for you. These experts can provide listings of local professionally led support group services in your area. A helpful resource to locate peer-led support groups is the National Alliance on Mental Health (NAMI), which

---

[140] Piper, Ogrodniczuk, Joyce, and Weideman, 2011

[141] Weir, 2018

can be accessed at nami.org/Support-Education/Support-Groups. See pages 113–114 for more general grief support resources.

GRIEF & SUICIDALITY: WHEN DARKNESS DROWNS ALL LIGHT

Grief is a normal and natural part of what it means to be human. For most, grieving is something that progresses naturally without the need for professional help. However, for many, dealing with loss may result in grief that is severe or prolonged, a grief that one just cannot seem to get over. When this occurs, seek professional mental health support without delay.

For some, grief may involve suicidality resulting from either their own thoughts of suicide or from someone else they know or care about who is considering, attempting, or has completed suicide. Suicidality is a difficult but important topic to discuss. Suicide kills more people each year than war, murders, and natural disasters combined.[142] *Re-read that last sentence and allow the statistical reality to soak in.* Suicidality is far too commonly a threat and far too little discussed.

Having open honest discussions about suicide is critical to our individual and collective health. It is time to bring suicide into regular appropriate conversations—including the talks we have in our homes with loved ones. Talking about suicide does not make someone suicidal. Talking about suicidality can help make sure you or someone you love receives needed help. It is essential that we, as a society, encourage understanding and supportive help for those impacted by suicide. If you or someone you know is thinking about suicide, contact a medical doctor or a mental healthcare professional now.

---

[142] American Foundation for Suicide Prevention, 2017

If you or someone you know is thinking about suicide, seek professional mental health support or contact the **Suicide & Crisis Lifeline.**

The Suicide & Crisis Lifeline is based in the United States, calls are toll-free, and someone is available to offer support 24/7. Those who are hearing impaired can text, chat, or dial 711 to reach the TTY relay service.

Dial 9-8-8 (available in multiple languages)
Text 988 (available in English only)
Chat 988lifeline.org/chat (available in English only)

Additional support can be found:

- The National Alliance on Mental Illness, nami.org
- American Foundation for Suicide Prevention, afsp.org

Chapter 7

STEP 5: ENGAGE IN THE NEW NORMAL

"In the end only three things matter: how much you loved, how gently you lived, and how gracefully you let go of the things not meant for you."

—BUDDHA

MOVING INTO THE LIGHT: FINDING THE NEW NORMAL

As explained in prior chapters, the grieving process is something that has no set time limits and no clear end-line. Inasmuch as grieving provides us a mechanism for healing from losses big and small, grief remains ever present in one form or another, whether we are currently grieving a loss or anticipating some loss to come. Since grief work is that mechanism for how we heal from our losses, why wouldn't we want this grief process to remain with us, healing and helping us our whole lives? Grieving is the process of healing from loss that we should invite into our every-day walking around life. In healthy grieving, grief finds a place in our life.[143] With normal integrated grief we learn to create a space for grief, inviting grief into our homes and setting a place for grief at our dinner tables.

---

[143] Center for Prolonged Grief, 2023

Grieving is a cyclical process that ebbs and flows throughout all our lives. It is like a breath we will breathe in and out daily throughout our lives. We do not one day magically stop grieving, so the question remains: how do we move forward after loss? We move forward *alongside* grief, in partnership with this amazing process for healing. Our final step in the grief process involves engaging in a "new normal" following a loss event, and a fine place to start is acceptance. The "new normal" life will also include adopting a livable pattern on grief work into its flow. One way to weave grief work into the fabric of our day-to-day is by utilizing the framework of the bio-psycho-social-spiritual model.

ACCEPTING LOSS: A STAGE, A PHASE, OR SOMETHING ELSE?

A healthy "new normal" after loss cannot be achieved without some level of accepting the loss. Allowing our brain and body time and space to acknowledge that the loss occurred can be difficult but is an essential step. This acceptance can often take time. For example, after each of my parents passed away years ago, I continued to find myself re-grieving their loss. In the months immediately following their deaths (which were separated by years), I found this re-grieving experience especially true. For example, I would be at a store and see a favorite item they liked and think for a brief second that I should buy it for them. Sometimes I would even catch myself literally reaching for the object only to be jolted back into the hard firm reality that they were no longer alive, and my reaching hand would fall, as would my crestfallen heart at the re-emergence of grief emotions. Although I clearly and fully realized my parents were gone (acceptance), at times, my brain went right back to denial, even if just for a few moments. In loss, this can be normal.

My father's death was sudden and too soon (he was only 48). I was young, just married, and living in a different city with my new husband at the time he passed. Even though I missed my family, I found myself wanting to go home less and less after his death. I had plenty of seemingly legitimate excuses as to why I would not be able to make it home for a visit, all of which sounded very logical to me at the time. In reality, there was something deeper driving my avoidance to return home. In my busy new world away from my father's house, I was not confronted with reminders of the reality of his death and at times it almost felt like he was still alive, even if just for a second. Part of me resisted facing the painful reality—he was gone. As a high school principal who was well-known and very socially engaged, his passing seemed to leave a hole felt throughout every corner of his small Texas community. During this time, returning home for visits meant facing not only my father's death, but also watching family I love and our community struggle with their grief pains. I was only 25 and ill-equipped at the time to handle any of this. Eventually, I learned to stop avoiding my home and family, and in doing so I was able to more fully lean into acceptance a little more deeply with each visit.

My experience is that acceptance of loss and the accompanying grief is not a stage or even a phase, but rather part of the cyclical process within grief work. Acceptance and re-acceptance can remain ongoing and, while acceptance/re-acceptance are part of grieving, these do not necessarily completely dissolve. Perhaps this can be understood by considering the difference between the terms "aggregate" and "amalgam." Some treat acceptance as an amalgam of grief, but I maintain it is an aggregate. Aggregate is a collection of different individual elements that gather into a whole, but even when combined, the individual elements remain. For example, if you pick up a piece of chipped concrete, you can see concrete is an aggregate—it is made up multiple individual elements that combine into one whole, but the chip reveals that the individual elements remain (you can still see flecks of grain, separate fragments of rock, etc.) remain. Amalgam is a mixture of different elements that combine to form one distinct new structure. The filling in my tooth, for example, is an amalgam of different materials that fully combined to create one new material. The grief process is aggregative in that there are different elements, including acceptance/re-acceptance, which combine and fold into grieving; however, these elements do not dissolve in the grieving process. Each element of grieving can remain distinct. As in the example of my father's death, acceptance for me was not a one-and-done activity that faded into a grief memory. My acceptance of my father's passing did not just dissolve, but rather remained distinct and continued to present itself again and again over time.

ACCEPTANCE: RE-EXAMINING THE STAGE MODEL

Accepting the loss is an important part of the process towards healing and re-healing. Much has been discussed (pros and cons alike) about the so-called grief stages, including the work of psychiatrist Elisabeth Kubler-Ross, in which the final "stage" is acceptance. While many contemporary mental health practitioners and researchers stiffen at the idea of grief having stages (me included), the premises brought forth by Kubler-Ross and others have been seminal and helpful for many grievers and for those who treat them. These traditional stages include: 1) denial, 2) anger, 3) bargaining, 4) depression, and 5) acceptance (DABDA). DABDA for many years was a primary grief model that became quite popular and familiar, yet recent findings from grief scholars have contradicted this stage process, calling into serious question its appropriateness and efficacy. Primary criticism of the stage model includes its lack of empirical evidence, it lacks clarity of concept (e.g., not every person will go through each of the so-called stages and, if they do, they may not experience them in their presented order), and it lacks explanation (the model should have been described as descriptive not prescriptive).[144]

---

[144] Stroebe, Shut, & Boerner, 2017

I agree that grief does not occur in stages and understand that the grief stage models have limitations; however, I depart from those who argue the stage models should be discarded and "relegated to the realms of history."[145] Instead, I suggest we not throw the metaphorical baby out with the bath water on this matter, but rather learn from the helpful insights and descriptors of grief brought forth by Kubler-Ross and others. A primary reason I am not ready to toss out DABDA is this simple truth: many of the people I work with still find much help from the model. Because the model had been previously so widespread, many come into counseling with familiarity of DABDA. Instead of advising these patients that the DABDA model, in which some find comfort, needs to be thrown out, I instead use that opportunity as an entry into grief work. Rather than dispelling and discarding DABDA, I can explain and expand on its premises, helping grievers understand grief does not occur in stages (it is cyclical), not everyone goes through each of the DABDA phases, and these phases are not necessarily liner (these can happen in any order and even some may co-occur simultaneously). Further, I can help grievers understand DABDA is not intended to be a one-and-done checklist; rather, these stages offer a guide for those struggling with loss, a glimpse of what potentially they may experience along their grief journey.

CONSTRUCTING A NEW NORMAL: THE BIO-PSYCHO-SOCIAL-SPIRITUAL FRAMEWORK

The bio-psycho-social-spiritual framework, incorporated into the GRACE Grief Model, is an important paradigm that can help us craft a new normal and construct a livable pattern of grieving that folds into our life in adaptive ways. Grief affects a person's cognitive, emotional,

---

[145] Stroebe, Shut, & Boerner, 2017, p. 455–456

and behavioral responses,[146] and these responses can influence the bio-psycho-social-spiritual framework of a person. Let us first understand what this term entails by examining its components' impacts: biological impact, psychosocial impact, social impact, and spiritual impact.

BIOLOGICAL IMPACT

Grief invites a generalized stress response (flight-flight-freeze-faint), which involves the cardiovascular system and the hypothalamic-pituitary-adrenal system. Research on bereavement reveals increases in catecholamines and cortisol even in the early stage of loss, yet this physical reaction to stress is not unique to bereavement in that it also mimics stress reaction in cases of other life events, such as job loss, natural disasters, etc.[147] Overall, the negative impact of grief adversely affects the immune system and promotes inflammation, which adversely effects cardiovascular functioning. Further, newer understandings about how genetics can be turned "off" and "on" is contributing to a growing correlation between stress exposure and grief, even theorizing genetics role in who does and does not develop prolonged grief or complicated grief.[148]

In addition to the neurobiological aspects, physical factors are also highly relevant in understanding grief, especially complicated grief. Research regarding complicated grief points to immunological variances that occur which can impact physical health. Combining "immunological and neuroimaging variables in bereavement research as one part of a multimethod approach will only increase our understanding of these (complicated grief) phenomena."[149] Grief has been associated with increased mortality and physical illness, including higher risks of car-

---

[146]   Shear et al., 2011

[147]   O'Connor, 2012

[148]   McCoyd & Walter, 2016

[149]   O'Connor, 2012, p. 146

diovascular disease, hypertension, high blood pressure, diabetes, chronic obstructive pulmonary disease.[150]

A person experiencing loss may develop psychosomatic reactions to that loss, which is often considered to indicate maladaptive coping.[151] As an example, grief can adversely impact physiology by sleep disturbances, notably insomnia. Insomnia in the grief process can be linked to post-loss depression.[152]

Not only can physical illness develop as a result of grief, but grief symptomology can conversely result from physical illness. This can create a loop: grief can result in physical illness; just as physical illness can result in grief. Bridges asserts physical pain resulting from major illnesses, such as cancer and heart disease, results in a unique grief and suggests counselors attune themselves to the grief that stems from physical illness.[153]

Viola's Panic Attack

Viola reached the hospital emergency room feeling as if she were dying. Her heart was pounding, she had shortness of breath, and she was experiencing dizziness, trembling, and tingling. Following examination, the doctor informed Viola that she was experiencing a panic attack. Viola could not believe it. She shared with the doctor that she had been feeling loss and anxiety since her husband was moved into an eldercare facility six months ago. Viola stated, "It can't be a panic attack, I didn't feel panicky all day and I actually felt pretty good that day." Viola did not realize that panic attacks, unlike anxiety attacks, come without warning. She soon after began professional counseling and, in time, Viola was able to minimize and manage her panic attacks and address her underlying grief.

---

[150] Spillane, Larkin, Corcoran, Matvienko-Sikar, & Arensman, 2017

[151] Gudmundsdottir, 2009

[152] Tanimukai et al., 2015

[153] Bridges, 2018

PSYCHOLOGICAL IMPACT

Grief affects mental wellbeing.[154] The psychological aspects of a person can be negatively affected following a loss event. In addition to complicated grief having the potential to exacerbate existing mental health conditions, having complicated grief is also linked to an increased risk of developing mental health issues such as depression, anxiety, and PTSD. Further, complicated grief's effects on mental wellbeing can cause disruptions in life functioning and contribute to life imbalances. Complicated grief also can lead the bereaved to isolate, self-neglect, or even self-harm.[155]

Grief's psychological impacts occur on a continuum of the loss response.[156] In normalized grief, psychological equilibrium is achieved relatively soon after the loss event, but in grief's more severe form, the psychological impacts can be more profound and detrimental.[157] In cases of complicated grief, the characteristic psychological impact includes anxiety, depression, avoidance, prolonged grieving, separation distress, emotional dysregulation, ruminations about the deceased or loss event, sense of emptiness and loss of meaning, inability to accept loss, and difficultly with overall life functioning.[158]

Hector's Complicated Grief

It had been six years since Hector's wife died of Alzheimer's. During her illness and subsequent to her passing, Hector continued to decline the many offers of help from family and friends. He was a proud man who struggled to share his feelings, but now years of unprocessed feelings

---

[154]   Maschi, Viola, Morgan, & Koskinen, 2015

[155]   Shear et al., 2011

[156]   Stroebe, Schut, & van den Boot, 2013

[157]   Stroebe, Schut, & van den Boot, 2013

[158]   Stroebe, Schut, & van den Boot, 2013

were beginning to cripple Hector's ability to function. He found himself withdrawing from others, no longer engaging in the hobbies he once loved, and even struggled to take care of himself. Hector explained that it was difficult for him to get through the day because all he could think about was his wife. Hector's once normal grief had digressed into prolonged grief, which required professional mental health support. However, Hector declined to get the professional help he needed, and so, sadly, Hector remained stuck in unprocessed grief as his mental and physical health continued to deteriorate.

SOCIAL IMPACT

Social relationships also change in relation to loss. For example, while positive social interactions are important to those dealing with grief, social dealings can be negative in the form of critical judging comments directed at the one experiencing a loss.[159] Even in societies that promote spiritual and religious freedoms, including freedom to choose how to grieve, bereaved people still often seek to be told what they should do and how they should feel with reference to grief.[160] Therefore, from an early age, children and youth are instructed how to think and act about grief, which extends even into adulthood.[161] This results in many adults dealing with bereavement left wondering what they are supposed to do and how they are supposed to feel.[162]

To address grief's social impact, there are increasing efforts towards creative activities that memorialize the deceased and support the mourning process.[163] Technology has changed the way many people interact, and

---

[159] Costa, Hall, & Stewart, 2007

[160] Parkes & Prigerson, 2009

[161] Parkes & Prigerson, 2009

[162] Parkes & Prigerson, 2009

[163] McCoyd & Walter, 2016

this extends to social interaction regarding grief.[164] With the decline in faith-based communal rituals, social platforms have become a new way to approach and address grief in the broader community. As an example, many are turning to Facebook and other Internet sites to express their grief.[165] Many websites are now targeted at promoting grief communities, including those creating virtual memories of a lost loved one (e.g., forevermissed.com; legacy.com, virtual-memories.com, etc.).[166]

Big Boys Don't Cry

Raymond was a child when his younger brother died suddenly in an accident. At the funeral, Raymond recalled watching his mother and the other women crying, yet he also noticed that no tears were shed by his father or the other men in his family. Raymond learned that day that "big boys don't cry," and he recalled how he trained himself thereafter to never cry. Years later, well into Raymond's adulthood, he still had not cried since the day of his brother's funeral. For Raymond this learned lesson was unhealthy. Not only had Raymond stopped years of tears, but he also learned to block years of emotions. It was not until Raymond read online about other men's similar grief response of blocking emotions that he realized he was not alone and found help. Raymond then joined a grief support group where he eventually learned to be vulnerable in healthy ways and, once again, allowed himself to feel and process his emotions.

---

[164] McCoyd & Walter, 2016

[165] Falconer, Sachsenweger, Bigson, & Norman, 2011; McCoyd & Walter, 2016

[166] McCoyd & Walter, 2016

SPIRITUAL IMPACT

Studies reveal a declining number of people are turning to traditional faith-based practices and rituals to address loss. An example is evidenced by fewer people in the U.S. and Europe are holding religious-based funerals.[167] For example, non-religious or ecumenical services of remembrance, such as those offered through hospice services, provide social opportunities of healing.[168]

Spiritualty can impact ones understanding of grief as well as provide coping resources and meaning in dealing with loss.[169] Spirituality is any way of relating to that which is sacred or to a greater reality.[170] Religion is a subset of the spiritual and involves culturally bound or institutional ways of relating to the sacred.[171] Many argue that the terms spiritual and religious should be separated.[172] However, for the purpose of this document, "spiritual" will remain the umbrella terminology within which matters of religion, faith, and beliefs will be discussed.

SPIRITUALITY IN PSYCHOTHERAPY

A growing body of evidence has suggested incorporating social aspects of religion and spirituality with attention to the individual's identity and relationship paradigms is helpful for a fuller investigation of the self within the psychotherapeutic relationship.[173] Research affirms religion and faith helps grievers, including those bereaved, by providing meaning

---

[167] Norton & Gino, 2014

[168] McCoyd & Walter, 2016

[169] Wortmann & Park, 2008

[170] Rosmarin, 2018

[171] Rosmarin, 2018

[172] Del Rio & White, 2012

[173] Tummala-Narra, 2009

and coping.[174] Those experiencing loss often turn to meaning-making within a spiritual context. In the case of bereavement, almost three-quarters of Americans believe in some form of afterlife.[175]

The topic of spirituality directly relates to most people in this country. Per a Gallup Poll conducted in 2022, 81 percent of Americans stated belief in God. Another study conducted in 2018 stated 80 percent of Americans affirm belief in God with three-quarters of American adults saying they talk (pray) to God or another higher power in the universe.[176]

Participation in spiritual practices, such as memorial services or sitting shiva, can provide an understanding of loss that includes meaning-making around loss and extends support through the grieving process to those impacted by the loss.[177] Other spiritual disciplines and practices, such as meditation and prayer (which can be individual or communal), also have been proven to provide help for those in grief by providing comfort.[178]

Brenda's Faith Family

Brenda grew up very close to her family, which included her parents and two brothers. As a child, she recalled weekly visits to the neighborhood church where she and her siblings would eagerly join their Sunday School class, excited to hear new Bible stories while being treated to cookies. Afterwards, all the kids would file into the sanctuary and sit alongside their friends or parents for worship. Years later, Brenda's developing career continued to take her further from home, ultimately moving her far away to live in other countries. While she very much enjoyed her job

---

[174] Matthews & Marwit, 2006

[175] Pew Research Center, 2022; Saad & Hrynowski, 2022

[176] Pew Forum, 2018

[177] Block, 2017

[178] Block, 2017

and exciting life abroad, Brenda often struggled with feeling lonely and dearly missing her family. This grief, at times, felt overwhelming. One day it occurred to Brenda that, while she may be oceans away from her own family, she could still allow herself to be with a faith family every week simply by visiting the local church where she now lived. Connecting into this new church, ableit a very different worship community than where she was raised, allowed Brenda to heal from feeling the loss of disconnection, while also promoting her individual spiritual growth.

The Example of Eve

Eve knew something had been wrong, and for a long time. She grew weary of feeling like her life was a yo-yo. At times, she battled bouts of severe depression that kept her from functioning normally, while at other times she felt like she had so much energy that nothing could stop her. Eve finally shared this with her doctor and was referred to a psychiatrist for evaluation. Soon after, Eve received a diagnosis of bipolar disorder. While part of Eve felt great relief finally knowing what the issue was, she also found herself struggling to accept the diagnosis (bipolar disorder is a mood disturbance that causes extreme mood swings that include emotional highs, as in mania or hypomania, and can cause lows, as in depression).

Eve began counseling and, in time, was able to recognize that she needed to grieve her diagnosis. Once given a diagnosis, many people find it difficult to accept, and Eve was no exception. We worked to help Eve understand her diagnosis and address the self-stigmatization she herself held on mental health issues.

Eve's psychiatrist monitored her new medications and treatment, during which time Eve learned in counseling therapy sessions the tools and techniques that she would need to better manage her bipolar swings and work through the grief that came with her new diagnosis.

She spent dedicated time and put great effort into her healing, including grief work. Eve was finally ready to find a new normal and move forward with her life. Eve used the GRACE Grief Model's step five as her guide, engaging in a "new normal" within a liveable pattern of grief work. With support, she was able to create a grief work plan for holistic healing by incorporating the bio-psycho-social-spiritual paradigm. Eve spent time working through the creation and implementation of her new comprehensive framework. The following lists a few of the highlights from Eve's new liveable grief plan:

- **Biological.** Eve's years of unresolved losses, including the grief around her mental health, had taken their toll on her physically. With therapy, she was able to understand the ways unresolved grief was affecting her body, and Eve made the choice to take positive action. For example, Eve realized she ate her feelings, meaning she turned to food to soothe. Years of self-medicating with food resulted in a large weight gain. Addressing feelings in healthier ways helped Eve stop overeating and deal with her grief.

- **Psychological.** Eve continued to work on her mental health with regular follow-ups with her psychiatrist and counselor. Medication prescribed by her psychiatrist helped balance Eve's moods and lessen her desire to self-medicate. With therapy,

Eve was able to learn how to open up and allow the grieving process in rather than avoiding it.

- **Social.** She realized the social/relational side of her life had suffered greatly due to untreated bipolar disorder. This often left her isolated and feeling much loss. With proper treatment and therapy, Eve was able to reengage with others in healthier ways.

- **Spiritual.** Eve grew up practicing the faith tradition of her parents, a faith she once valued greatly. However, beginning at age 19 years she began drifing away from her family's spiritual practices. Now, Eve decided to re-incorporate some of her prior faith practices into her life and, specifically, into her bipolar treament plan. For Eve, adding practices, such as meditation and prayer, provided for her much comfort and proved to be helpful tools.

Chapter 8

LEAVING THE HARBOR: A FINAL WORD

"Real grief is not healed by time…If time does anything, it deepens our grief. The longer we live, the more fully we become aware of who she was for us, and the more intimately we experience what her love meant for us. Real, deep love is, as you know, very unobtrusive, seemingly easy and obvious, and so obvious that we take it for granted. Therefore, it is often only in retrospect—or better, in memory, that we fully realize its power and depth. Yes, indeed, love often makes itself visible in pain."

—Henri Nouwen

LEAVING THE HARBOR

How tempting it may feel at times for us to remain where we are in the grieving process and not move forward. This, however, can keep us stuck in grief, stuck in an imagined safe harbor where we are lulled into believing familiar feelings of grief are comfortable and normal, creating for us a false sense of safety in which we fail to progress and heal. "A ship in harbor is safe, but that is not what ships are built for."[179] True

---

[179] Shedd, 1928

healing from loss most often requires that we allow ourselves to leave perceived comfort areas, encouraging ourselves to be authentically and appropriately vulnerable in processing loss narratives. To heal, one must venture into the difficult waters of grief work, learning to live into a new normal while allowing ourselves to continue to heal and re-heal by the grief processes.

Previously, you learned how each of us are wonderfully made; every person has been formed out of flesh and bones, but also out of star-dust.[180] Every person's body is made up of atoms that are billions of years old,[181] and these bodies are hard-wired with insight and intuition that is formed in part from the DNA that shapes us. Each body has innate wisdom, and that innate wisdom includes insight and intuition designed to help us heal.

When our bodies are injured, they are hard-wired to try and heal themselves. While at times we may need support for our healing processes, the body is still remarkably adept at trying to mend itself. This innate healing process includes our body's attempt to recover from losses. Losses are a natural and inevitable part of every life, like a thread that weaves in and out of our life's narrative. The body is wonderfully created to heal from losses through the process we call grieving.

STUCK IN THE HARBOR: A STORY OF LOSS FROM MISCARRIAGES

We are, indeed, hard-wired for grief work. However, in today's West-ernized world, it seems we have been de-programed from many healthy innate ways of grieving, and too often culturally indoctrinated to regard loss and grief as largely something to minimize or avoid altogether. As an example, when I suffered four miscarriages at different stages of

---

[180] Schrijver & Schrijver, 2015
[181] Schrijver & Schrijver, 2015

pregnancy over several years, each time I was left devastated and hurting physically and emotionally. Despite the reality that pregnancy loss is incredibly common, I found only one of my acquaintances who even spoke of it. However, because of cultural programming and my own delayed grief response, I did not speak of it, leaving me unable to move forward in my grief journey. In my personal loss, there was no holding the babies or saying goodbye, there were no funerals for these little souls, there was no show of compassion or support to walk alongside me. I was stuck, as many others also have experienced, wounded by sorrow, and left with no way to grief and no one to grieve with.

After each of my four difficult losses, I experienced many fine people offering regretfully unhelpful and too often hurtful comments, such as "it was for the best," "don't worry, you'll have other pregnancies," or "your babies are angels in heaven now." I also noticed people avoided me following each miscarriage. Very few people asked me how I was doing, and even fewer even spoke of my miscarriages. At this time in my life, I learned a damaging lesson, which was not to talk about or think about the loss. From my personal experience, and in my work as a minister and professional counselor, I know pregnancy losses remain still mostly unspoken and, therefore, remain mostly ungrieved.

My miscarriages occurred while living in a major metropolitan city with ample resources for support, yet I sought out no help initially. Eventually realizing I did indeed need help, I began combing libraries and bookstores in search of books on miscarriage. After hours spent in the city's two largest bookstores, I found rows and rows of books on how to get pregnant, how to handle pregnancy, and what to do when baby arrives. Sadly, I was only able to locate two books about miscarriage. I remain grateful I did, at least, find two. Since that time, I am very pleased to share that I now see more and more books every year published on the topic of pregnancy loss, and most are easily obtainable online.

When I read my two books about miscarriage, I learned of other cultures that openly discuss and deal with pregnancy loss in adaptive, healthy ways. I was filled with hope to find other traditions that not only did not minimize this type of loss but offered open support and healing for all those involved in these tragedies. One tradition in particular I recall reading about centered on stories coming from Japan referencing a particular Buddhist practice called *mizuko kuyo*, "water child memorial service."[182] *Mizuko kuyo* is a type of ceremony acknowledging deaths by miscarriage, abortion, and stillbirth. In Buddhist temples, shrines are made of small statues representing *mizuko Jizo* (water child Buddhas), each statue representing the soul of a deceased baby or fetus. Upon further research and seeing pictures of row-upon-row of the tiny Jizo statues, I found myself saddened by the countless little lives lost and knowing that each of those lives meant there were walking-wounded trying to deal with those losses. But in these images, I also found comfort in knowing I was not alone in my grief, and I found great hope that I could maybe find my own type of *mizuko kuyo*. Years later, I did find my own type of memorial service when I worked with my church to create and conduct a service open to all for those grieving from the loss of a pregnancy.

Not talking about my miscarriages often felt like the safest option, which became my false "safe harbor." However, not talking about the losses and failing to process my feelings of grief only prolonged my pain. It took years (and therapy) before I was able to realize just how much I needed to speak about the deaths of my unborn babies. It took years before I ventured into the difficult waters of the grieving process and began to allow myself to feel waves of loss, ultimately finding comfort in the healing waters of grief.

---

[182] Klass & Heath, 1997

�֎ CONCLUDING COMMENTS

I WISH TO EXTEND TO you, the reader, a personal note of thanks for going on this grief journey with me. Grief has taken me on a deeply personal and humbling path, one which I continue taking steps on daily. My hope for you is that you allow grief to be a companion for healing. May you use the energy from waves of loss to carry you into the healing waters of grief work. Here, you are met with opportunity to re-story and recover, to mend wounds and to progress forward with hope and continued restoration. The creation of the GRACE Grief Model and this book represents a labor of love spanning many years. I created this grief model out of necessity in an attempt to offer those struggling with loss a new evidenced-based way of healing that includes elements of cognitive behavior therapy and narrative therapy within a framework that supports individual beliefs, goals, and sense of purpose (including spirituality). It is my sincere hope and prayer that the information shared in this book supports your healing processes to recover from loss and lean into a renewed healthy normal.

I hope you have benefited from the GRACE Grief Model and encourage you to embrace the concept that grief is good, grief will ebb and flow, and grief is a gift. The work of grief is how we heal from loss. With each loss you address, you have the opportunity to grow, to learn, and to heal. Your efforts can create processes of healthy grieving as a life pattern, a pattern of being and becoming, moving you deeper into healing and closer to your hopeful future story and a sense of peace, shalom.

At the completion of this book, I invite you to take a moment to appreciate the commitment of time and effort made towards healing. Working through grief takes time, hard work, and courage. The "Certificate of Grief Work Progression" provided on the next page is one way to acknowledge and mark this accomplishment.

To further support you along your grief journey, I have created an additional resource, *GRACE: A Model for Grieving Workbook* to serve as a complementary tool to this handbook. The GRACE Workbook expands the information within this text and offers a wealth of supportive tools and exercises that align with the GRACE Grief Model to move you even further towards health and healing.

✳ THE GRACE GRIEF MODEL CERTIFICATE OF GRIEF WORK PROGRESSION

ACKNOWLEDGING YOUR PROGRESS AND marking the successful completion of this book can be an important way to affirm your healthy grieving process as you journey forward.

On this date _____, I _____
celebrate my forward progress in my grief journey. As part of this journey, I have successfully completed this book, *GRACE: A Model for Grieving*.

I also affirm:

- Grief is a journey that takes time. I will be patient with myself, as healing takes time. I will remember that slow progress is still progress.

- Grief is good because, when we grieve in healthy ways, grief is how we heal from loss. Therefore, I commit to embracing healthy ways to grieve and I invite the grieving process into my life today and every day.

- Grief is cyclical and I acknowledge that grief will ebb and flow.

- Grief is a gift because, as we grieve in healthy ways, grief allows me to grow as I heal from loss.

- I will allow myself to continue writing my loss stories and also remember to re-write them (enrichen the narratives to include fuller, honest, and accurate descriptions, including positive aspects that allow me to move forward and heal).

- I am now and will continue to move forward in my grieving process. I give myself full permission to heal.

- I will continue to allow others to support and help me on my journey. We were created to grieve in community.

- I am healing! I understand the reality of loss never goes away, but that my understanding can grow and my painful feelings can heal. I will continue to move forward.

> "Grief can be the garden of compassion. If you keep your heart open through everything, your pain can become your greatest ally in your life's search for love and wisdom."
>
> —RUMI

✤ ACKNOWLEDGEMENTS

THE PEOPLE TO WHOM I owe much are many. While I may not be able to list every person in acknowledgement of their supportive teaching and mentoring which helped guide my professional career, I do wish to express my sincerest gratitude to the following whose contributions to my work during the formation and practicing of the GRACE Grief Model have been immense. These people not only shaped me as a practitioner, but their advice and support helped me create and practice a new grief model, moving my casual ideas into thoughtfully informed instruction, thus aiding me in making this book a reality. Thank you Dr. Lauren Marangell, Dr. Rayan Al Jurdi, and the entire team at Brain Health Consultants and TMS Center. I also sincerely thank Dr. Jerry Terrill, Rev. Ann Spears, Dr. Lorna Bradley, Dr. Dawn Ellison, and Rev. Salvador Delmundo Jr.

Additionally, I extend a heartfelt appreciation to my patients and clients who allow me the privilege of walking alongside them on their grief journey. They have each taught me so much. It is my honor to work with them, and I am in awe of their courage.

Finally, I wish to extend special acknowledgment to everyone on my publishing team for their vision and tremendous support of this work. Thank you for helping me share valuable grief support with so many people in need.

✳ RESOURCES

Substance Abuse and Mental Health Services Administration (SAMSHA)

samhsa.gov/find-help/national-helpline

National Alliance on Mental Health (NAMI)

nami.org

The Center for Loss and Life Transition

centerforloss.com

What's Your Grief

whatsyourgrief.com

Mindfulness and Grief Institute

mindfulnessandgrief.com

Bo's Place (for adults, children, and youth)

bosplace.org

Dougy Center (for children and youth)

dougy.org

Actively Moving Forward (for young adults)

healgrief.org/actively-moving-forward

Bereaved Parents

bereavedparentsusa.org

Hope for Widows

hopeforwidows.org

National Widowers Organization

nationalwidowers.org

The Montrose Center (LGBTQ+ support)

montrosecenter.org

National Center for School Crisis and Bereavement

schoolcrisiscenter.org

The American Foundation for Suicide Prevention

afsp.org

The Shared Grief Project

sharedgrief.org

Mental Health Gateway

mentalhealthgateway.org

✳ ABOUT THE AUTHOR

Kay Towns, DPC, LPC, is a licensed professional counselor and mental health advocate. She earned her doctorate in Professional Counseling from Mississippi College, a master's degree in counseling from Houston Graduate School of Theology, and a master's degree in theological studies from Southern Methodist University. She completed her clinical training at one of the  top psychiatric hospitals in the U.S., The Menninger Clinic in Houston, Texas. Kay is also an ordained minister in The United Methodist Church. Her therapeutic approach is to provide support and feedback to help people grow from their struggles, heal from their pain, and move forward towards their hopeful future story.

✳ REFERENCES

Ali, S., Rhodes, L., Moreea, O., McMillan, D., Gilbody, S., Leach, C., Lucock, M., Lutz, W., & Delgadillo, J. (2017). How durable is the effect of low intensity CBT for depression and anxiety? Remission and relapse in a longitudinal cohort study. *Behaviour Research and Therapy*. 94: p 1–8.

Altena, E. & Chen, I. & Daviaux, Y. & Ivers, H. & Philip, P. & Morin, C. (2017). How hyperarousal and sleep reactivity are represented in different adult age groups: Results from a large cohort study on insomnia. *Brain Sciences*. 7. DOI: 10.3390/brainsci7040041.

American Foundation for Suicide Prevention (2023). afsp.org/.

American Psychiatric Association (2022). *Diagnostic and statistical manual of mental disorders* (5th ed., text rev.). DOI: 10.1176/appi.books.9780890425787.

Ansari, M.F.U.R. (1970). *The qur'anic foundations and structure of Muslim society* (1). Indus Educational Foundation.

Baardseth, T.P., Goldberg, S.B., Pace, B.T., Wislocki, A.P., Frost, N.D., Siddiqui, J.R., Lindemann, A.M., Kivlighan, D.M. 3rd, Laska, K.M., Del Re, A.C., Minami, T., & Wampold, B.E. (2013). Cognitive-behavioral therapy versus other therapies: redux. *Clin Psychol Rev. Apr;33*(3):395-405. DOI: 10.1016/j.cpr.2013.01.004.

Barley, N. (1997). *Dancing On the Grave: Encounters with Death*. Abacus.

Barrett, L.F., & Satpute, A.B. (2013). Large-scale brain networks in affective and social neuroscience: towards an integrative functional architecture of the brain. *Curr. Opin. Neurobiol.* 23, 361–372. DOI: 10.1016/j.conb.2012.12.012.

Betz, G., & Thorngren, J. M. (2006). Ambiguous loss and the family grieving process. *The Family Journal, 14*(4), 359–365. DOI: 10.1177/1066480706290052.

Bitbrain (2019). What are emotions and feelings, and how to measure them. bitbrain.com/blog/difference-feelings-emotions

Block, S. (2017). *Grief and Loss: A guide to preparing for and mourning the death of a loved one.* Harvard Health Publishing.

Boelen, P.A., & de Keijser, J. (2007). Treatment of complicated grief: A comparison between cognitive behavior therapy and supportive counseling. *Journal of Consulting and Clinical Psychology, 75*(2), 277-284. DOI: 10.1037/0022-006X.75.2.277.

Boss, P. (2016). The context and process of theory development: The story of ambiguous loss. *Journal of Family Theory & Review,* 8, 269-286. DOI: 10.1111/jftr.12152.

Bridges, R. (2018). Hearing the grief in illness and pain. *Therapy Today, 29*(3), 36-39.

Bristowe, K., Marshall, S., & Harding, R. (2016). The bereavement experiences of lesbian, gay, bisexual and/or trans* people who have lost a partner: A systematic review, thematic synthesis and modelling of the literature. *Palliative Medicine,* 30(8),730-744. DOI: 10.1177/0269216316634601.

Brown, B. (2019. *Daring Greatly: How the Courage to Be Vulnerable Transforms the Way We Live, Love, Parent, and Lead.* Penguin.

Burton, R. (2019). Our brains tell stories so we can live. *Nautilus,* April 6. nautil.us/our-b rains-tell-stories-so-we-can-live-237501/.

Cashwell, C. S., & Young, J. S. (Eds.). (2011). *Integrating Spirituality and Religion into Counseling* (2nd ed.). American Counseling Association.

Costa, B.M., Hall, L. & Stewart, J. (2007). Qualitative exploration of the nature of grief-related beliefs and expectations. *Omega: Journal of Death and Dying, 55*(1), 27-36. DOI: 10.2190/CL20-02G6-607R-8561.

Center for Prolonged Grief (2023). prolongedgrief.columbia.edu.

Chen, Z., Ying, J., Ingles, J. *et al.* (2020). Gender differential impact of bereavement on health outcomes: evidence from the China Health and Retirement Longitudinal Study, 2011– 2015. *BMC Psychiatry* 20, 514. DOI: 10.1186/s12888-020-02916-2.

Chiu, Y., Yin, S., Hsieh, H., Wu, W. Chuang, H., & Huang, C. (2011). Bereaved females are more likely to suffer from mood problems even if they do not meet the criteria for prolonged grief. *Psycho-Oncology, 20,* 1061–1068. DOI: 10.1002/pon.1811.

Cuijpers, P., van Straten, A., Andersson, G., & van Oppen, P. (2008). Psychotherapy for depression in adults: A meta-analysis of comparative outcome studies. *Journal of Consulting and Clinical Psychology.* 76 (6), 909–922. DOI: 10.1037/a0013075.

Damasio, A. (1999). *The Feeling of What Happens: Body and Emotion in the Making of Consciousness.* Harcourt College Publishers.

Damasio, A. & Carvalho, G. (2018). The nature of feelings: evolutionary and neurobiological origins. *Nat Rev Neurosci* 14, 143–152 (2013). DOI: 10.1038/nrn3403.

David, D., Cristea, I. & Holmann, S.G. (2018). Why cognitive behavioral therapy is the current gold standard of psychotherapy. *Frontiers in Psychiatry*, 9,4. DOI: 10.3389.fpsyt.2018.00004.

Davis, C.G., Wortman, C.B., Lehman, D.R., & Silver, R.C. (2000). Searching for meaning in loss: are clinical assumptions correct. *Death Stud.* Sep;24(6):497-540. DOI: 10.1080/07481180050121471.

Del Rio, C.M., & White, L.J. (2012). Separating spirituality from religiosity: A hylomorphic attitudinal perspective. *Psychology of Religion and Spirituality, 4*(2). DOI: 10.1037/a0027552.

Deng, Y., Chang, L., Yang, M., Huo, M., & Zhou, R. (2016). Gender differences in emotional response: Inconsistency between experience and expressivity. *PLoS ONE, 11*(6). DOI: 10.1371/journal.pone.0158666.

Dixon, M. (2023). Does the amygdala hijack your brain? *Psychology Today,* January 3, 2023. https://www.psychologytoday.com/us/blog/202301/does-the-amygdala-hijack-your-brain.

Doka, K. J. (Ed.). (1989). *Disenfranchised Grief: Recognizing Hidden Sorrow.* Lexington Books/D. C. Heath and Com.

Doran, G., & Hanson, N.D. (2006). Constructions of Mexican American family grief after the death of a child: An exploratory study. *Cultural Diversity and Ethnic Minority Psychology, 12,* 199–211. DOI:10.1037/1099–9809.12.2.199.

Dulwhich Center (2023). dulwichcentre.com.au/collection-evidence-for-the-effectiveness-of- narrative-therapy/.

Durà-Vilà, G., Littlewood, R., & Leavey, G. (2013). Integration of sexual trauma in a religious narrative: transformation, resolution and growth among contemplative nuns. *Transcult Psychiatry.* Feb;50(1):21-46. DOI: 10.1177/1363461512467769.

Easwaran , E. (2007a). *The Bhagavad Gita: Introduced & translated by Eknath Easwaran ,* (2nd ed.). Nilgiri Press.

Easwaran , E. (2007b). *The Dhammapada: Introduced & translated by Eknath Easwaran ,* (2nd ed.). Nilgiri Press.

Eckman, P. (1972). Universal and cultural differences in facial expression of emotion. *Proceedings of the Nebraska Symposium on Motivation, 19,* 207–284. Lincoln: University of Nebraska Press.

Elinger, G., Hasson-Ohayon, I., Bar-Shachar, Y., & Peri, T. (2023). Narrative reconstruction therapy for prolonged grief disorder: Basic interventions and mechanisms of change. *Death Stud.* Jan 6:1-12. DOI: 10.1080/07481187.2022.2164633.

Enez, O. (2018). Complicated grief: Epidemiology, clinical features, assessment and diagnosis. *Current Approaches in Psychiatry, 10*(3), 269-279. DOI: 10.18863/pgy.358110.

Epston, D. (1992). Experience, contradiction, narrative & imagination: selected papers of David Epston & Michael White, 1989-1991. Adelaide: Dulwich Centre.

Falconer, K., Sachsenweger, M., Gibson, K., & Norman, H. (2011). Grieving in the Internet age. *New Zealand Journal of Psychology, 40*(3), 79-88.

Franco, M., & Yang, N. (2020). Culture impacts how we grieve. *Psychology Today*, April 27. psychologytoday.com/us/blog/platonic-love/202004/culture-impacts-how-we- grieve.

Frankel, E. (2014). The edge of grief: A summer reflection. *Huffington Post.* huffpost.com/entry/the-edge-of-grief-a-summe_b_5604156.

Goldberg, C. (1998). Cognitive-behavioral therapy for panic: Effectiveness and limitations. *Psychiatry Q* 69, 23–44. DOI: 10.1023/A:1022181206728.

Gour. S.H.S. (1929). *The spirit of Buddhism.* Luzac and Co.

Gross, J. J. (2013). Emotion regulation: Taking stock and moving forward. *Emotion, 13*(3), 359– 365. DOI: 10.1037/a0032135.

Gudmundsdottir, M. (2009). Embodied grief: Bereaved parents' narratives of their suffering body. *Journal of Death and Dying, 59*(3), 253-269. DOI: 10.2190/OM.59.3.e.

Hamilton, I.J. (2016). Understanding grief and bereavement. *Br J Gen Pract.* Oct;66(651):523. DOI: 10.3399/bjgp16X687325.

Heelas, P. (1986). Emotion talk across cultures. In Harre, R. (ed.),*The Social Construction of Emotions*, Basil Blackwell. 234–266.

Henningsen, Peter. (2018). Management of somatic symptom disorder. *Dialogues in Clinical Neuroscience.* 20. 23-31. DOI: 10.31887/DCNS.2018.20.1/phenningsen.

Hill, C. (2018). *Meaning in Life: A Therapists Guide.* American Psychological Association.

Ho, S.W., & Brotherson, S.E. (2007). Cultural influences on parental bereavement in Chinese families. *OMEGA: Journal of Death & Dying,* 55, 1–25. DOI:10.2190/4293-202 l-5475- 2161.

Hofmann, S.G. (2021). The future of cognitive behavioral therapy. *Cogn Ther Res* 45, 383–384. DOI: 10.1007/s10608-021-10232-6.

Hofmann, S.G., Asnaani, A., Vonk, I.J., Sawyer, A.T., & Fang, A. (2012). The efficacy of cognitive behavioral therapy: A review of meta-analyses. *Cognit Ther Res.,* Oct 1;36(5):427-440. DOI: 10.1007/s10608-012-9476-1.

Holmes J. (2002). All you need is cognitive behaviour therapy? *BMJ,* Feb 2;324(7332):288-90; discussion 290-4. DOI: 10.1136/bmj.324.7332.288.

Humberman, A. (Host). (2022, May 30). The science and process of healing from grief (Audio podcast). Stanford School of Medicine. hubermanlab.com/the-science-and-process- of-healing-from-grief/.

Ito, M., Nakajima, S., Fujisawa, D., Miyashita, M., Kim, Y., Shear, M.K., Ghesquiere, A., & Wall, M.M. (2012). Brief measure for screening complicated grief: Reliability and discriminant validity. *PLoS ONE,* 7(2), e31209. DOI: 10.1371/journal.pone.0031209.

Iwamasa, G. Y., & Hays, P. A. (2019). *Culturally responsive cognitive behavior therapy: Practice and supervision.* American Psychological Association.

Kandel, E. (2018). *The Disordered Mind: What Unusual Brains Tell Us About Ourselves*, Farrar, Straus and Giroux.

Kateregga , B.D. , & Shenk , D.W. (1981). *Islam and Christianity: A Muslim and a Christian in dialogue*. William B. Eerdmans Publishing Company.

Kersting, A., Brahler, E., Glaesmer, H., & Wagner, B. (2011). Prevalence of complicated grief in a representative population-based sample. *Journal of Affective Disorders, 131*(1-3), 339-343. DOI: 10.1016/j.jad.2010.11.032.

Kersting, A., & Kroker, K. (2009). Prolonged grief as a distinct disorder, specifically affecting female health. *Archives of Women's Mental Health* (2010) *13*, 27–28. DOI: 10.1007/s00737-009-0112-3.

Klass, D., & Heath, A.O. (1997). Grief and abortion: Mizuko Kuyo, The Japanese ritual resolution. *OMEGA - Journal of Death and Dying, 34*(1), 1-14. DOI: 10.2190/NVP6-4FL4-JTE7-BBK2.

Lathrop D. (2017). Disenfranchised grief and physician burnout. *Ann Fam Med*. Jul;15(4):375-378. DOI: 10.1370/afm.2074.

Lim, N. (2016). Cultural differences in emotion: differences in emotional arousal level between the East and the West. *Integr Med Res*. Jun;5(2):105-109. DOI: 10.1016/j.imr.2016.03.004.

Linde, K., Treml, J., Steinig, J., Nagl, M., & Kersting, A. (2017). Grief interventions for people bereaved by suicide: A systematic review. *PLoS One*. Jun 23;12(6):e0179496. DOI: 10.1371/journal.pone.0179496.

Lindquist, K. A., & Barrett, L. F. (2012). A functional architecture of the human brain: emerging insights from the science of emotion. *Trends Cogn. Sci*. 16, 533–540. DOI: 10.1016/j.tics.2012.09.005.

Maciejewski PK, Maercker A, Boelen PA, Prigerson HG (2016). "Prolonged grief disorder" and "persistent complex bereavement disorder", but not "complicated grief", are one and the same diagnostic entity: an analysis of data from the Yale Bereavement Study. *World Psychiatry.* Oct;15(3):266-275.

Maercker, A., & Znoj, H. J. (2010). The younger sibling of PTSD: Similarities and differences between complicated grief and posttraumatic stress disorder. *European Journal of Psychotraumatology,* 1, 19. DOI:10.3402/ejpt.v1i0.5558.

Maschi, T., Viola, D., Morgan, K. & Koskinen, L. (2015). Trauma, stress, grief, loss, and separation among older adults in prison: the protective role of coping resources on physical and mental well-being. *Journal of Crime and Justice, 38*(1). DOI: 10.1080/0735648X.2013.808853.

Matthews, L.T., & Marwit, S.J. (2006). Meaning Reconstruction in the Context of Religious Coping: Rebuilding the Shattered Assumptive World. *OMEGA - Journal of Death and Dying, 53*(1), 87–104. DOI: 10.2190/DKMM-B7KQ-6MPD-LJNA.

McCoyd, J., & Walter, C. (2016). *Grief and Loss Across the Lifespan*, Springer Publishing.

McCreight B.S. (2004). A grief ignored: Narratives of pregnancy loss from a male perspective, *Sociology of Health & Illness, 26*(3): 326–50. DOI: 10.1111/j.1467- 9566.2004.00393.x.

Miyabayashi, S., & Yasuda, J. (2007). Effects of loss from suicide, accidents, acute illness and chronic illness on bereaved spouse and parents in Japan: Their general health, depressive mood, and grief reaction. *Psychiatry and Clinical Neurosciences, 61,* 502-508. DOI: 10.1111/j.1440-1819.2007.01699.x.

Moayedoddin, B., & Markowitz, J.C. (2015). Abnormal grief: Should we consider a more patient-centered approach? *American Journal of Psychotherapy, 69*(4), 361-378.

Montano, S.A., Lewey, J.H., O'Toole, S.K., & Graves, D. (2016). Reliability generalization of the Texas Revised Inventory of Grief (TRIG). *Death Studies, 40*(4), 256-262. DOI: 10.1080/07481187.2015.1129370.

Morin, C. (2002), Contribution of cognitive-behavior approaches to the clinical management of insomnia, *Primary Care Companion, Journal of Psychiatry, 4*(sup 1). psychiatrist.com/wp-content/uploads/2021/02/24316_contributions-cognitive- behavioral-approachesto-clinical.pdf.

National Alliance on Mental Illness (2023). nami.org/.

Nakajima, S. (2018). Complicated grief: recent developments in diagnostic criteria and treatment. *Philosophical Transactions Royal Society B*, 373. DOI: http://dx.doi.org/10.1098/rstb.2017.0273.

Neimeyer, R.A. (1999). Narrative strategies in grief therapy. *Journal of Constructivist Psychology, 12*, 65-85. DOI: 10.1080/107205399266226.

Neimeyer, R. A., & Currier, J. M. (2009). Grief therapy: Evidence of efficacy and emerging directions. *Current Directions in Psychological Science, 18*(6), 352–356. DOI: 10.1111/j.1467-8721.2009.01666.x.

Norton, M. & Gino, F. (2014). Rituals alleviate grieving for loved ones, lovers, and lotteries. *Journal of Experimental Psychology, 143*(1), 266–272. DOI: 10.1037/a0031772.

Nouwen, H. (2009). *A Letter of Consolation*. HarperOne.

O'Connor, M.F. (2012). Immunological and neuroimaging biomarkers of complicated grief. *Dialogues in clinical neuroscience, 14*(2), 141-8. DOI:10.31887/DCNS.2012.14.2/mfoconnor.

O'Connor, M. (2022). *The Grieving Brain*, Harper One.

O'Connor, M.F., Wellisch, D.K., Stanton, A.L., Eisenberger, N.I., Irwin, M.R. & Lieberman, M.D. (2008) Craving love? Complicated grief activates brain's reward center. *NeuroImage* 42:969–72. DOI: 10.1016/j.neuroimage.2008.04.25.

Okon-Singer, H., Hendler, T., Pessoa, L., & Shackman, A. (2015). The neurobiology of emotion– cognition interactions: fundamental questions and strategies for future research. *Frontiers in Human Neuroscience, 9.* DOI: 0.3389/fnhum.2015.00058.

Park, C.L. (2010). Making sense of the meaning literature: An integrative review of meaning making and its effects on adjustment to stressful life events. *Psychological Bulletin, 136,* 257–301.

Park, C.L. (2011). Implicit Religion and the Meaning-making Model. *Implicit Religion, 14,* 405- 419.

Park, C.L. (2013). The meaning-making model: A framework for understanding meaning, spirituality, and stress-related growth in health psychology. *The European Health Psychologist, 15*(2), 40-45.

Park, C.L. (2017). Distinctions to promote an integrated perspective on meaning: Global meaning and meaning-making processes. *Journal of Constructivist Psychology,* 30(1), 14-19, DOI: 10.1080/10720537.2015.1119082.

Park, C.L. (2020). Religiousness and meaning-making following stressful life events. *The Science of Religion, Spirituality ,and Existentialism,* Chapter 19, 273-285, DOI: 10.1016/B978-0-12- 817204-9.00020-2.

Park, C. L., Edmondson, D., & Hale-Smith, A. (2013). Why religion? Meaning as motivation. In K. I. Pargament, J. J. Exline, & J. W. Jones (Eds.), *APA Handbook of Psychology, Religion, and Spirituality (Vol. 1): Context, Theory, and Research* (pp. 157–171). American Psychological Association. DOI: 10.1037/14045-008.

Park, C.L., & Halifax, R.J. (2011). Religion and spirituality in adjusting to bereavement: Grief as burden, grief as a gift. In R.A. Neimeyer, D.L, Harris, H.R. Winokeur, & G.F. Thornton (Eds.), *Grief and Bereavement in Contemporary Society.* Routledge.

Parkes, C.M., & Prigerson, H.G., (2009). *Bereavement: Studies of grief in adult life* (4th edition). London, England: Routledge.

Pargament, K.I. (1997). *The Psychology of Religion and Coping*. Guilford.

Payne, A. (2024). Sermon: "Forgive and Forgiven."

Pessoa, L. (2013). *The Cognitive-Emotional Brain: From Interactions to Integration*. MIT Press. DOI: 10.7551/mitpress/9780262019569. 001.0001

Puña Vargas, C.I., Armaiz-Pena, G.N., & Castro-Figueroa, E.M. (2021). A Biopsychosocial approach to grief, depression, and the role of emotional regulation. *Behavioral Sciences, 11*, 110. DOI: *10.3390/bs11080110*.

Pew Forum (2018). pewforum.org/wp-content/uploads/sites/7/2018/04/Beliefs-about- God-FOR-WEB-FULL-REPORT.pdf.

Pew Research Center (2022). *Beliefs on afterlife*. pewresearch.org/religion/2021/11/23/views-on-the-afterlife/.

Prakash, S. (1985). *Hindu religion and morality*. Asian Publication Service.

Ratnayake, S. & Poppe, C. (2022). Ethical issues in cognitive-behavioral therapy, in Manuel Trachsel and others (eds), *Oxford Handbook of Psychotherapy Ethics* (2021; online edn, Oxford Academic, 4 Oct. 2019), DOI: 10.1093/oxfordhb/9780198817338.013.43.

Raz, G., Jacob, Y., Gonen, T., Winetraub, Y., Flash, T., Soreq, E., et al. (2014). Cry for her or cry with her: context-dependent dissociation of two modes of cinematic empathy reflected in network cohesion dynamics. *Soc. Cogn. Affect. Neurosci. 9*, 30–38. DOI: 10.1093/scan/nst052.

Rosmarin, D. (2018). *Spirituality, Religion, and Cognitive-Behavioral Therapy*. Guildford Press.

Rosner, R., Pfoh, G., & Kotoučová, M. (2011). Treatment of complicated grief. *European Journal of Psychotraumatology, 2*. DOI:10.3402/ejpt. v2i0.7995.

Rye, M.S., Pargament, K.I., Ali, M.A., Beck, G.L., Dorff, E.N., Hallisey, C.,... Williams, J.G. (2000). Religious perspectives on forgiveness. In M.

E. McCullough, K. I. Pargament, & C. E. Thoresen (Eds.) *Forgiveness: Theory, research, and practice.* New York: Guilford Press, p. 17–40.

Saad, L, & Hrynowski, Z. (2022, June 24). How many Americans believe in God. Gallup. news.gallup.com/poll/268205/americans-believe-god. aspx#.

Scheff, T. (2015). What are emotions? A physical theory. *Review of General Psychology, 19*(4), 458-464. DOI: doi.org/10.1037/gpr0000058.

Schmitter, A. M. (2014). 17th and 18th century theories of emotions, in *Stanford Encyclopedia of Philosophy*, ed. E. N. Zalta (Stanford, CA: Stanford University). http://plato.stanford.edu/entries/emotions-17th18th/.

Schneck, N., Tu, T., Haufe, S., Bonanno, G.A., Galfalvy, H., Ochsner, K.N., Mann, J.J., & Sajda, P. (2019). Ongoing monitoring of mindwandering in avoidant grief through cortico-basal- ganglia interactions. *Soc Cogn Affect Neurosci.* Feb 13;14(2):163-172. DOI: 10.1093/scan/nsy114.

Schrijver, K., & Schrijver, I. (2015). *Living with the Stars: How the Human Body Is Connected to the Life Cycles of the Earth, the Planets, and the Stars.* Oxford Press, Oxford, UK.

Shear, M. K. (2011). Bereavement and the DSM-5. *Omega: Journal of Death and Dying, 64,* 101–118. DOI: http://dx.doi.org/10.2190/OM.64.2.a.

Shear, K., Simon, N., Wall, M., Zisook, S., Neimeyer, R., Duan, N., Reynolds, C., Lebowitz, B., Sung, S., Ghesquiere, A., Gorscak, B., Clayton, P., Ito, M., Nakajima, S., Konishi, T., Melhem, N., Meer, K., Schiff, M., O'Connor, M., First, M., Sareen, J., Bolton, J., Skritskaya, N., Mancini, A.D., & Keshaviah, A. (2011). Complicated grief and related bereavement issues for the DSM-5. *Depression and Anxiety, 28*(2), 103–117. DOI:10.1002/da.20780.

Shedd, J. (1928). *Salt from My Attic*, The Mosher Press, Portland, Maine; cited in *The Yale Book of Quotations* (2006) ed. Fred R. Shapiro, p. 705; there are numerous variants of this expression.

Shott, S. (1979). Emotion and social life: A symbolic interactionist analysis. *American Journal of Sociology, 84*(6), 1317-1334. DOI: 10.1086/226936.

Simon, N.M. (2013). Treating complicated grief. *JAMA, 310*(4), 416-23.

Spillane, A., Larkin, C., Corcoran, P., Matvienko-Sikar, K., & Arensman, E. (2017). What are the physical and psychological health effects of suicide bereavement on family members? Protocol for an observational and interview mixed-methods study in Ireland. *British Medical Journal, 7,* 1-8. DOI:10.1136/bmjopen-2016-014707.

Stelzer, E.M., Zhou, N., Maercker, A., O'Connor, M.F. & Killikelly, C. (2020) Prolonged grief disorder and the cultural crisis. *Front. Psychol,* 10:2982. DOI: 10.3389/fpsyg.2019.02982.

Stroebe, M., Schut, H., & Boerner, K. (2017). Cautioning health-care professionals: Bereaved persons are misguided through the stages of grief. *OMEGA, Journal of Death and Dying, 74*(4) 455–473. DOI: 10.1177/0030222817691870 journals.sagepub.com/home/ome.

Stroebe, M., Schut, H., & van den Boot, J. (2013). *Complicated Grief: Scientific Foundations for Health Care Professionals.* New York: NY, Taylor and Francis.

Tanimukai, H., Adachi, H., Hirai, K., Matsui, T., Shimizu, M., Miyashita, M., & Shima, Y. (2015). Association between depressive symptoms and changes in sleep condition in the grieving process. *Supportive Care in Cancer, 23*(7), 193501931. DOI: 10.1007/s00520-014- 2548.

Thimm, J.C., & Holland, J.M. (2017). Early maladaptive schemas, meaning-making, and complicated grief symptoms after bereavement. *International Journal of Stress Management, 24*(4), 347-367. DOI: 10.1037/str0000042.

Thompson, B.E., & Neimeyer, R.A. (2014). Thompson, B. E., & Neimeyer, R. A. (Eds.). (2014). Grief and the Expressive Arts: Practices for Creating Meaning. *OMEGA - Journal of Death and Dying, 72,* 362-365. DOI: 10.1177/0030222815598047.

Timmins L., Pitman A., King M., et al. (2023). Does the impact of bereavement vary between same and different gender partnerships? A representative national, cross-sectional study. *Psychological Medicine.* 53(9):3849-3857.

Torpy, J.M., Burke, A.E., & Golub, R.M. (2011). Panic disorder. *JAMA,* Mar 23;305(12), 1256. DOI: 10.1001/jama.305.12.1256. PMID: 21427380.

Tottenham, N., & Gabard-Durnam L.J. (2017). The developing amygdala: a student of the world and a teacher of the cortex. *Curr Opin Psychol,* Oct.17, 55-60. DOI: 10.1016/j.copsyc.2017.06.012.

Tummala-Narra, P. (2009). The relevance of a psychoanalytic perspective n exploring religious and spiritualty identity in psychotherapy. *Psychoanalytic Psychology, 26*(1), 83-95. DOI: 10.1037/a0014673.

Tyler, J.M., & Darrow, N.T. (2022), The impact of cultural resiliency on traumatic loss, *Counseling Today,* January 2023, 40-45. ct.counseling. org/2023/01/the-impact-of-cultural- resiliency-on-traumatic-loss/.

Vesnaver E., Keller H.H., Sutherland O., Maitland S.B., & Locher J.L. (2016). Alone at the table: Food behavior and the loss of commensality in widowhood. *J Gerontol B Psychol Sci Soc Sci.* Nov. 71(6),1059-1069. DOI: 10.1093/geronb/gbv103.

Walker, A.C. (2008). Grieving in the Muscogee Creek tribe. *Death Studies, 32,* 123–141. DOI:10.1080/07481180701801238.

Webb, J.R., Toussaint, L. & Conway-Williams, E. (2012): Forgiveness and health: Psycho-spiritual integration and the promotion of better healthcare. *Journal of Health Care Chaplaincy, 18* (1-2), 57-73. DOI: 10.1080/08854726.2012.667317.

White, M., & Epston, D. (1990). *Narrative means to therapeutic ends.* New York, NY: Norton.

Williams-Reade, J., Freitas, C., & Lawson, L. (2014). Narrative-informed medical family therapy: Using narrative therapy practices in brief medical encounters. *Families, Systems, & Health, 32*(4), 416-425. DOI: 10.1037/fsh0000082.

Worden, W.J. (2018). *Grief Counseling and Grief Therapy: A handbook for the mental health practitioner* (5th edition). New York, NY: Springer Publishing.

Wortmann, J.H., & Park, C.L. (2009). Religion/spirituality and change in meaning after bereavement: Qualitative evidence for the meaning-making model. *Journal of Loss and Trauma, 14*(1), 17-34. DOI: 10.1080/15325020802173876.

NOTES

NOTES

NOTES

NOTES

NOTES

NOTES

NOTES